"No one who engages Dr. Meeks's life th⌐ want to live her life. She tells her story truth-telling. Everyone who engages Dr. Meeks's life through her memories will make her story their own, transforming their lives into solidarity with the oppressed, joining the battle against white supremacy."

—**Eduard Loring,** The Open Door Community

"In this deeply empathetic and compelling book, Dr. Catherine Meeks—the doyenne of truth-telling—stitches together the pieces of her life, creating brave space from which to share her experiences and wisdom as healer, teacher, and spiritual leader. We are fortunate to be able to hear her story as she wants to tell it, and to be inspired to tell our own stories with the 'scraps of love' from our own lives."

—**Jerlena Griffin-Desta,** coauthor of *Facing You, Facing Me*

"*A Quilted Life* is the memoir of a remarkable human being called to become a prophetic witness. Dr. Catherine Meeks's story offers us a look at the fabric of faithfulness and provides careful readers with essential wisdom and courage for their own journey toward justice."

—**David Fleer,** independent scholar

"In this remarkable story, Catherine Meeks takes us to the far reaches of our life together—places where most souls would not dare go alone. Her great gift to the reader is her compassionate sense of courage! Put your hand in hers and let her take you there."

—**Reverend Tom Brackett,** The Episcopal Church

"Decades before she was 'Dr. Meeks,' she was my dearest friend 'Cathy.' We met at Pepperdine and came of age together. We talked about boys, family, our future careers. But on the night of March 12, 1969, our world was shattered into pieces and our innocence stripped away. Reading this memoir will provide a true understanding of how my friend went from mild-mannered 'Cathy' to the beautiful, iron-willed, and fearless 'pioneer of racial healing'—Dr. Catherine Meeks. Read with the knowledge that you, too, can evolve."

—**Cookye Rutledge,** Young Scholars Academy

"This mesmerizing autobiography is the account of an extraordinary Black woman's battle to free herself and others from the biases that gave birth to slavery and still haunt us. Written with a candor about herself, her family, and her faith that avoids rationalization and recrimination, this is the story of a quilt whose pieces include the hues of achievement and pain. I cannot recommend it strongly enough."

—**Gregory E. Sterling,** Yale Divinity School

"The magnificence of *A Quilted Life* is its quiet blues rhythm, its obeisance to Black rural, southern culture, its beautifully simple sentence structure, which holds the heart and mind of a mighty Black woman. This is a memoir for the ages, revealing how and why Black people survived. If you read it, your soul will be made glad."

—**Daniel Black,** Clark Atlanta University,
author of *Black on Black*

"This is her story, this is her song, and what an amazing journey! *A Quilted Life* is a candid account of a life shaped by juxtapositions and informed by a faith-filled and fierce determination to find her own voice, see beauty in a racist world, and be well. With the skill of a master artisan, Meeks's evolving sense of self provides a glimpse of what might be possible when we see ourselves for who we are and exercise courageous faith to navigate life on our terms."

—**Angela D. Sims,**
Colgate Rochester Crozer Divinity School

A QUILTED LIFE

Reflections of a Sharecropper's Daughter

Catherine Meeks

WILLIAM B. EERDMANS PUBLISHING COMPANY
GRAND RAPIDS, MICHIGAN

Wm. B. Eerdmans Publishing Co.
4035 Park East Court SE, Grand Rapids, Michigan 49546
www.eerdmans.com

Book design by Lydia Hall

Printed in the United States of America

30 29 28 27 26 25 24   1 2 3 4 5 6 7

ISBN 978-0-8028-8289-9

Library of Congress Cataloging-in-Publication Data

A catalog record for this book is available from the Library of
Congress.

To my parents, Sidney Meeks Sr.
and Malissa Alberta Jackson Meeks,
and to Dr. Ross M. Miller Jr.

Contents

Foreword

Dr. Catherine Meeks and I have lived two distinctly separate but similar lives, separated by era, geography, and lineage. But as her memoir reflects, we are remarkably intertwined.

Our paths are quilt-like undertakings. Quilting is the fabric of combination! Combination of patterns, textures, stories, and styles. Two days after I was born, I came into a household where quilting was the basis of connection. My newly found Grantee was the matriarch of a family that took me in; quilting was her solace, and watching her became mine.

Catherine's upbringing was much the same: quilting sewed together not just people, places, and things but also memories and lessons. And I think there could not have been a more perfect union between two souls than through a metaphor meant to comfort and cover in a time most urgent in the need of restoration.

My connection with Dr. Meeks stands from a serendipitous encounter between a patient and a doctor.

She, in need of surgery, was recommended to a young physician by her brother. That surgeon was my father.

Dr. Ross Miller became her mentor, employer, and encourager. I'd like to think he pointed an already motivated and brilliant young woman in a direction in which she could catch lift and soar!

It is clear to me that the people whom you encounter in life, both positive and negative, often have the ability to point you in the direction of your trajectory. And my dad was one of those people who gave Dr. Meeks exposure to consciousness and insight that she may not have fully recognized.

She might never have had the opportunity to share this origin story with me if I had not taken a risk to tell my own story on CBS News, following the murder of George Floyd in June 2020. A friend of hers watched and shared and connected us. What a gift!

Dr. Meeks was able to share so much of my own family story, my father—so much I never knew—without judgment! It encapsulates her own journey and her own ability to see, feel, and forgive.

Her life is a life lived well. It's impossible *not* to recognize.

Dr. Meeks's mission is simple: to open dialogue not only for racial equity but for allyship, harmony, and truth.

And she is seen as one of the preeminent soldiers in the field of justice.

Reading her memoir is reading the history of ourselves. It is connecting the dots to our own humanity, our own purpose, and it gives us power and strength in our ability to do something to ensure that our lives matter.

Our meeting was such an incredible serendipitous opportunity! We provided one another with connection, completely unaware of each other's existence, and yet so much have we been on the same path.

I salute Dr. Catherine Meeks and not only what she has achieved but what she seeks to continue to do!

We all should. And we should all delve into her story!

Michelle Miller
Cohost of CBS Saturday Morning

Preface

M Y MOTHER, WHO WAS A QUILTER, kept a rag sack. When I learned what these rags were, I found that they were not just pieces of cloth, but pieces of love that were taken from the old clothes we had owned and loved until they were worn out. Looking at those pieces of cloth, they didn't look like much. They were faded and thin, discolored through use and age. Their distinctive textures were worn down. Their colors were ghosts of what they once had been. Some people might've looked at them and thought them worthless. But that couldn't be further from the truth. Mama's rag sack contained the contents that would become the small, pieced-together squares, triangles, stars, and other geometric shapes that formed large, patterned quilt tops. After the tops were made, they were sewn together with a back lining to hold a cotton filling that gave them weight, since they were being made to keep us warm and not simply for beauty. Those rags had the capacity to transform and to be transformed, just as all our inner and outer experiences transform us.

My memories of my mother's quilting have helped me frame the story of my long life's journey. This journey began in a black walnut grove, where I ran around in the late

1940s as a free-spirited little girl on my grandfather's one hundred acres of homesteaded land in Junction City, Arkansas. I was the daughter of a sharecropper, and I often worked in the fields myself. I witnessed my father's desperation and endured life in segregated small towns. And yet, my journey continued on. I walked through the halls of major universities and distinguished myself as an academic, despite having a father who could not read or write. I traveled to West Africa, connecting with its rich culture and history. I served in offices of municipal government, fighting for those people often forgotten by the powerful. Finally, my journey led to the pulpit where Dr. Martin Luther King Jr., former Secretary of State Madeleine Albright, *New York Times* columnist David Brooks, Archbishop Desmond Tutu, and Presiding Bishop Michael Curry had stood to preach. I preached at Washington National Cathedral, using the only voice I have ever had. Although it took me many years to find this voice, it is now respected nationally and internationally, demanding liberation for oppressed people everywhere. I have worked through many fears to find this voice. And now it is a voice that continually declares that brave space, not "safe space," is what we have to create in the racial healing arena.

My journey resembles quilt making in that it comprises many experiences that the world would see as raggy—irredeemable or useless. I have suffered from rheumatoid arthritis and have been exhausted by trying to build a career in racist institutions. I have raised two Black young men, on my own, in a country that threatens the lives and safety of Black men. Despite the hardship, each of these experiences has allowed me new opportunities to listen for the sound of the genuine in myself and in the world around me. The rags became more than mere rags. They are threads of love that were waiting to be put into conversation with one another.

Pieced together, they would be transformed into a beautiful whole. All the disparate emotions, fears, hopes, dreams, successes, and failures that may seem worthless actually hold massive potential to help in creating something new that never existed before.

In the quilting world, nothing is useless, because the quilter's imagination allows her to see beyond what is in her rag sack. She knows that all the rags that she has carefully harvested for quilting day can be used to make new shapes and borders for the quilt that she is imagining. This is also the case in the journey from birth to death. It is sometimes difficult to believe that all things work together for good. However, this makes more sense to me when I find a way to let go of having to declare that all things *are* good. Sometimes bad things happen. I have suffered a wide variety of wounds on this journey, and the pain is real. I am not particularly interested in martyrdom, because I prefer not to suffer, but a life begun in a sharecropping world cannot be without suffering and pain.

As an adult, it took me a long time to understand that sharecropping is merely glorified slavery. My father worked as a sharecropper all his life. His love for the land and his ability to nurture whatever he grew into productivity were phenomenal. Still, my father succumbed to the weight of desperation that was inherent to living under this glorified slavery. These two pieces of cloth—my father's love of the land, and my father's desperate economic position—sit next to each other in the quilt.

I have been marginalized, denigrated, and traumatized by the narratives of systemic racism. I have been subjected to lies about white superiority and Black inferiority. I have suffered from the competition among those of us who are impacted in the systems of denigration, who seemingly have never known—or forgotten the importance of—standing in solidarity with one another. It has been a daily struggle to hold on to hope while navigating the serious desperation caused by anti-Black racism. I have seen how our country reinforces the oppression of the past, even as it congratulates itself for having made progress. I have been the rare or designated Negro who managed to escape some of the carefully designed and managed snares of oppression. This, too, is another piece of the quilt. It is a piece that many would consider ugly—and those people would be right. But next to this piece sits the determination of the spirit to be free. Systemic racism does not get to have the last word, just as the rag sack is not the last word for the old clothes that have had the salvageable parts torn from them and saved for a new day.

This racist world had plans for me that my soul did not accept. Even as a young child, I refused to sit in the dimly lit waiting room that was designated for Black patients. I had to walk past the well-lit, well-furnished spaces prepared for the white patients. I could see the effects of segregation, and I refused to accept them. I never mumbled a word about what I was doing, and actually I am not sure that I knew what I was doing. But something in me knew I had to resist, that this system of segregation was not how things should be, and though I had to wait in that dimly lit space, I did not have to sit, which I never did. The pathway to being a resister, and someone who is willing to tolerate the disruption that comes from this resistance, was forged at some unknown point for me years ago. I was able to hold on to hope regardless of the daily doses of desperation. This hope stitched the edges of the scraps that I collected in my sack.

I traveled from the safe walnut grove that sheltered me in my early years, although I had no idea what was awaiting me. As a young girl, I experienced fears that I had no language for. These fears, caused in part by racism, swirled above me like the Arkansas storms. As a teenager, I was not sure that the world wanted me. Further along my journey, I began to find my voice as an academic and an activist. I learned to say, "Make space, because I intend to stay." Now I am a wise older woman, a crone, no longer overshadowed by fear. I stand without apology or doubt. I know I was meant to come here and that I have something to do while walking this path. If rags could think and feel, they would know there is more for them. But it doesn't matter, because the quilter knows what the plan is for those pieces. No matter how long it takes to get to the actual work of making the quilt, the vision of the new entity is never lost. This is the way hope manifests itself in the souls of the oppressed people who know they were meant to be free.

This book invites you, the reader, to take off your shoes and join me on the journey. We'll visit my grandfather's black walnut grove, and the sharecropping cotton fields that my father managed. You'll see what it was like to inhabit substandard schoolrooms without crayons, books, and other basic supplies. You'll also witness the educational opportunities that helped my bright young mind to thrive. You'll see how I learned to think about what others were saying while also determining what my own thoughts were. The journey continues with my work in a mayor's office, having accepted the challenge to wage a local, national, and international campaign against racism and violence. Then it extends to the shores of West Africa, where I finally realized that I could dance when invited onto the dance floor by the right partner. Along the way are glimpses of my ongoing search for a deeper understanding of myself. All these pieces of my journey are pieces of love, waiting to be stitched together, to be made into something beautiful. Some of the colorful rags are filled with sorrow, whereas others hold joy, and many are wrinkled by fear. Some of them are worn by the same repeated struggles—struggles with finding self-acceptance and deep self-love. They are stitched alongside other scraps: my self-discovery through dreams, journaling, creative endeavors, and spiritual life. These scraps all bear testimony to what is possible for a little Black girl from Arkansas, searching for a place to be a well person.

This book invites you, the reader, to find your places to enter into this story. You can hear what resonates with your own quest for freedom and wellness as you wiggle your toes in the shoes of my experience, shaped by an ongoing struggle with chronic illness that includes a thirty- eight-year struggle with rheumatoid arthritis, hip joint replacements, and fibromyalgia. You are invited to reflect on what it is like to be a single mother trying to manage such illness while raising a teenager and a preteen with too few financial resources. I hope you will find it generative to notice the threads of faith and my stubborn unwillingness to allow external circumstances to dictate my life. As you walk a few miles with me in the pages ahead, pay attention to all that is unsettled in your heart and the questions that have arisen around that. Listen for the sound of the genuine and discern how it applies to your own life. My story bears witness to the fact that being focused and faithful matters in the long run. What rags have you gathered that can be unified through focus and faith? How do your physical ailments contribute to a beautiful life story? How can your struggles be sewn together to make something new?

This is my story, and I have tried to tell it as clearly as possible without involving those who are closest to me in any manner that might cause them angst or concern. It remains to be seen if that goal is achieved. But I have been careful. My siblings are purposefully left unnamed, as are my parents. My life was impacted by them and continues to be, and I am grateful for them. I am also grateful for my sons, who will tell their own story in whatever manner they choose as they navigate the intricacies of their lives. This is my story. These are my observations and analyses. It has not been easy to plot the story's course and to find the best way to characterize my thoughts on all those plot points. But I hope that my telling of this journey—the sharing of the contents of my rag sack—might encourage, inspire, challenge, bring hope, spark imagination and creativity, open a heart door, or lead a reader forward.

Living my life, and writing this book, has taken courage. To sew together my story quilt, I've gathered every piece of love available, every scrap, wanted and unwanted. And now I offer that quilt to you with humility and hope.

1

Awakenings

I WAS BORN IN 1946 AND SPENT my first five years of life in Junction City, Arkansas. This town might have had five hundred people in it, but I'm not sure anyone ever bothered to count. The size of the town did not matter to my family or me. We lived in a house at the end of a dirt road, on a small portion of the one hundred acres that my grandfather had homesteaded. He paid a small fee for the land and agreed to live on it for at least five years. It is amazing that he had managed to learn that this was possible. Once he found the opportunity, his agency allowed him to take advantage of it.

There was no world for me beyond two houses and the small stretch of land between them. We lived in my uncle's former house. (He had moved to another part of the state to live with his wife.) There were multiple black walnut trees in a small grove separating that house from the one where my grandfather and aunt lived. The great joy for me was that I could make my way back and forth between the two houses whenever I felt like it. I was not afraid as I traveled between them, and no one was worried for me. My little world was safe, and I had no name for fear because I never felt it. There was no way, then, for me to know that these carefree days would not last forever.

My mother was a beautiful woman who I think did not realize that about herself. She was creative and a courageous folk medicine person. Mama's creativity led her to make lovely clothes from the chicken and pig food sacks that she faithfully saved—she turned the sacks into blouses, skirts, and dresses for my sister and me, and shirts for my brother. She loved to put lace collars on our dresses and to decorate the fronts of our blouses with many tiny tucks. She made meals that turned out to be feasts when it didn't appear that there was much food around. Even when our pantry was empty, we found surprising Sunday dinners waiting for us after she had been in the kitchen most of the day. She made the best desserts using whatever she had. She would make a potato pie using white potatoes if she didn't have sweet potatoes, or she would make a cobbler dough, simply add butter, spices, and sugar, and bake it, calling it a "butter roll." She had a wonderful imagination and was tenacious about making the best out of difficult situations. She always seemed to believe what she said about any troubling day: "tomorrow is another day, and you don't know what it will bring." She had hope, and it kept her moving ahead toward the life she imagined for herself. From my mother, I learned that education is the best key to unlocking the prison doors of racism and poverty. And that it did not matter how long it took to get an education or how much hardship you had to go through; it was worth it. My mother would go to school throughout my childhood; I was eighteen when she graduated from college. When I was young, I had no idea how hard and long my mother would toil to get her college degree, nor how deeply etched the message of getting an education would become in my soul.

My father possessed an intuitive understanding of the land, and his connection to it was sustaining for him. My father loved farming. He would rise before sunup to go walk around the cotton field, surveying what had happened during the night. I could never understand what he was trying to see. It would take me years to understand the value of the lessons he taught me through this practice. From him, I came to learn that the person who wishes to grow something successfully has to pay attention. It is important to be watchful and to learn all that you can about what the land needs in order to thrive.

My father was not formally educated because he had to help his own father with farming duties. As a result, he did not have a chance to go to school. Even though Daddy couldn't read or write, he loved to hear me read when I was a little girl. He never turned down the invitations I gave him to listen to me read, which reinforced my desire to read and to read well. He would sit patiently with me on his lap as I read to him for hours. He didn't talk to me about what I read. Instead, he listened, and that was all that mattered to me. I loved to go with him when he needed to sign the yearly farming agreement document with the white men whose land we lived on. He sharecropped this land, and the agreement document codified the awful arrangement. Daddy would take me to the store where all the business was conducted. There, a bunch of white men would sit around watching us. He would make his X, and then I would get to write his name. I was proud to be able to help him. It never occurred to me that I was able to show off my writing because he was not able to write. While I have no idea how he must have felt having to take his little girl with him to write his name, I realize now that he rarely went to church with us, and part of the reason for that may have been to avoid the embarrassment of not being able to read in the Sunday school classes we had. I don't really know, but I wonder.

My birth certificate says my mother was thirty-two and my father was fifty-two when I was born. I know Mama got married late, late according to the cultural expectations at the time. Before she married, she found work in the homes of white women when there were no teaching assignments for women who had not finished college. She lived with my grandfather and her sisters. My father's first wife died before I was born, and I don't know anything about her. He had seven children with her, who had mostly grown up and moved away by the time I was born.

My father was an unlettered sharecropper, who thought each year that things would get better, but they never did. The sharecropping system was designed to make sure that the Black folks who were living on the land of white folks and working that land for a portion of the yearly earnings never had any money left when they finished paying for everything. The sharecropper had to pay for a portion of the seeds, fertilizer, and any other costs associated with raising the crop. In addition, the food for a sharecropper's family and farm animals was purchased from the white landowner, who also owned a general store. All these things were sold on credit, and at the end of the farm year, when the cotton was harvested, the settlement was made and all those bills were paid. There was usually no money left to be given to the sharecropping family, so the cycle began again. This was what my father faced for his entire life.

Our house wasn't equipped with all the modern conveniences—we had outside toilets and wells—but that was of no concern to me. I was a little girl who lived in a playland that existed between our house and my grandfather's house. In this playland I could visit the pigs, help collect eggs, watch my aunt churn milk into butter, pick fresh vegetables from the garden, try to shell peas, or just ramble around outside, watching the sky, doing nothing whatsoever but being a little girl. A favorite pastime for me was watching my grandfather make baskets and mend broken-down furniture.

My grandfather was a basket weaver and a repairer of chairs. He used strips made from small white oak trees to make baskets, placing the strips in tubs of water to soak until they were pliable enough to weave. He also used these strips to replace the bottoms of chairs. He kept all his supplies in the black walnut grove. I often watched him work and wondered what on earth he was doing. He didn't talk to me much but didn't seem to be bothered by having me as an observer. We had several of his creations in our house, and there were many in the house where he and my aunt lived, across the black walnut grove. From my grandfather, I learned that you can make things with your hands and that you can fix things with them also. He would stay out in the grove all day working, and as he did, it was fun to sit with him in silence. I had no idea that I was learning so much about silence—and about being content with what is before you to do—from sitting with this old gentleman who worked, as if his livelihood depended on it, at a task that he was doing simply because he loved the craft and artistry.

Besides watching my grandfather do his work, I loved exploring the house where he lived with my aunt. My aunt was not married and had no children, but she was always kind and generous toward my siblings and me. I had such a feeling of freedom and adventure when I went to visit her. She had a large bed with a feather mattress. I loved to dive into it and get swallowed by the soft feathers as I sank into them. This felt like magic to me. Like I had floated away. My aunt made her bed very carefully each morning. She did not seem to mind that, in my fun, I was messing it up. She never scolded me and actually seemed amused.

I also had fun exploring my aunt's kitchen and often got into things that were potentially dangerous. One morning I reached for an object of curiosity and knocked over a can that contained fat drippings, rendered from the bacon and fatback we cooked each day. I spilled the warm grease onto myself and was surprised by its slimy, sticky feel. Fortunately, it was late morning, so the grease was no longer hot enough to burn my skin.

Another high adventure involved the new wringer washing machine that my aunt had purchased. I was fascinated by this new gadget. One day, while trying to see how it worked, my hand got caught. Since my hand was small, it went right through the wringer, the gears grinding my small bones. I screamed from the shock. Thankfully, I did not break any bones. I wasn't punished for this, nor for the many other times I got into things that I should have left alone. Mostly I was told not to do it again, and my family let it go.

This was my early world. I had the freedom to travel to and from my grandfather's house at will. I enjoyed my aunt's tea cakes and cookies and sifting through her jewelry boxes. My aunt was a teacher, but she was a farm woman as well. She would teach all day, and then when she came home, she'd take care of her animals and cook. She had cows, chickens, pigs, and a garden. She was up before daylight every day, doing animal chores, and then back in the house, getting ready to go to school as the sun came up. When all her other tasks were finished, she would retire to her room to do schoolwork. She never said anything about how much work she was doing. But I was puzzled about it when I watched her milk the cows and churn their milk into butter. I wondered if I would have to get up in the dark someday, like her. My grandfather was in his eighties when I was born; thus, he was not able to do all the caretaking that was necessary to maintain their mini-farm. My aunt never complained about all the work she did. She made it all seem very natural.

For the first five years of my life, the fears of the larger world never encroached on the world of my black walnut grove. I am sure the adults in my life—my mother, father, grandfather, and aunt—were facing very real fears. They were also haunted by even more frightening memories of the past, though they never talked about them, and it would be years later that I would come to hear any such stories. In these first few years there was nothing to introduce me to the hounds of racism.

My first conscious experience of fear was when I was five years old. My mother found a teaching job in Moro, Arkansas, which was 186 miles from Junction City. Moro had a population of less than two hundred. Both Moro and Junction City were hardly more than wide spots on the road, sprinkled with a few houses. They both had only a general store and a farm supply store. There were no streetlights and only one paved road. Not many African Americans were visible in either one of these towns because folks lived on farms in the rural areas, and most African Americans lived on the surrounding farms. We made requisite visits to the stores to purchase whatever goods could not be raised or created on our farms.

Mama was hired to teach first grade at George Washington Carver School. Our all-Black segregated school was located on Highway 79, and the students were brought there by bus every day from the surrounding farms. This school, like most segregated schools at that time, was the recipient of the white school's hand-me-down books and chalk. The white school was located in the part of our little town primarily populated by white people three miles away, and each year the old books and half-used chalk sticks would be brought to Carver for us to use. I didn't know about this until I began to go to school at age six, a year after we arrived in Moro, Arkansas, for the first time.

The job began in late October 1951. It would go until early December and then break for a few months. This was because the school year was organized into what were called split terms to accommodate farmers and the harvesting seasons.

My mother and I went to this strange place, leaving my father, brother, and sister back in Junction City. I did not understand why I had to go. I guess it was too much for my father to manage the three of us kids. The day my mother and I left for Moro, I thought about hiding so they could not find me when it was time to go. I was overwhelmed by the fear of the unknown. I had never been anywhere except to El Dorado, which was seventeen miles from Junction City. I could not imagine what this long trip might be like. Because I had no way of naming this new experience, fear overtook me. I had names only for the two houses, the space between them, the walnut grove. I had no idea what to expect when we got to the place we were going. It sounded as if it could be close to the moon, because I was told, once I was in the car, that it would take most of the day to get there. My uncle drove us. It seemed as if we would never get there, but we finally arrived at a small house of strangers who were to become our landlords.

In Moro, my mother and I were roomers with a family. Mama was a roomer instead of a boarder. This meant she had to cook our meals, but she made arrangements with the landlady to babysit me during the day while she was teaching because I was not in school yet.

After we arrived and settled in, I learned that I was going to have to stay with these strangers during the day while Mama was at school. This was a terrible idea. I did not know these folks. The house was big and seemed to have endless rooms—which I doubt as I think about it now. I think it was my frightened little five-year-old heart that imagined it as such a huge place. I thought about running away so that I could avoid the whole ordeal of being left with them. After more thinking, I decided that running away was not the best idea because it was cold there. Instead, I decided to awake early enough each morning to ask Mama not to leave me. However, that plan failed because I always woke up too late, and she was already gone. I developed the habit of waking up to see if Mama's coat was on the back of the door. When it wasn't there, I knew I had missed her again. I would lie there, quietly crying for as long as I could stand to stay in that room alone. Finally, I would decide that I had to leave our room and see if anyone was going to take care of me. Of course, they did. I was well taken care of, with the landlady preparing my breakfast and seeing to my getting dressed, and everyone being very nice to me. Still, I could not get free of the fear. Every morning it was as if I'd forgotten how kind the landlady had been to me the day before. I was overwhelmed by the fear of being alone, without my mother, and I can't remember how I spent my days other than that I was always watching for Mama to return.

Each night before my mother and I went to bed, I was deeply afraid of waking and seeing my mother's coat gone. I imagined that one afternoon, she would go to work and never come back. I imagined what it would be like to be in that boarding house, waiting for my mother, only to never see her again. I didn't know how I would get back to the rest of my family if she didn't come back. This place was certainly not my black walnut grove. There were no feather mattresses to sink into, no tubs of Grandpa's white oak strips to survey. I missed seeing the chickens, cows, and pigs. I wanted to be able to roam around instead of having to just sit in a room with strangers. I wanted to play with my brother and sister. I wanted to sit on Daddy's lap again and listen to him tell us ghost stories before bed.

One day, to my great surprise, Mama informed me that we were going back to Junction City because the school where she taught was going to be closed for a bit. It did not occur to me that we would be moving back to Moro again in January. We were going home to our little house, and I would see the rest of my family, see the black walnut grove. This was the only thing that concerned me.

Shortly after Christmas, I learned that when we returned to Moro, the whole family—my father, brother, and sister—would be coming with us, and later my older half sister would join us for a part of the school year because she was a long-term substitute teacher. I was glad that we were all going together. Knowing that my family would be together made all the difference. It would not be just Mama and me, alone in a strange place. My fear of the unknown transformed into a keen sense of adventure. This time, when we left, I sat in contentment between my uncle and my mother in the front seat of a moving truck. I looked behind me eagerly, catching a glimpse of the car behind us. I knew another uncle was driving that car, and that my father and siblings were riding along. My little heart was joyful about the possibilities waiting for us. This time, all of us were doing this trip together. There would be no more lonesome mornings, waking up, looking for Mama's coat.

We rented a three-room house situated right off Highway 79. This stretch of highway divided Moro's houses from the general store and George Washington Carver School, so we had to cross the busy highway to get to school or to the store. The house had no indoor plumbing, no grass in the yard, and a very old-fashioned pump in the back, which required us to pour water into it to prime it each time we wanted to pump from it. We had to pump any water we needed for baths, dishes, or drinking. It took a good amount of time to pump enough water to meet all our water needs. The woman we rented from appeared to be Native American. I'm not sure about that because I had never seen anyone who looked like her before. She had long black hair and very beautiful, brown, leathery skin. She lived next door in a bigger house with her sons and several other people, but their house didn't look much different from ours. She was always kind to us. There were two or three houses in the vicinity that were painted white, and the contrast between them and where we lived was quite stark to me. Our house was unpainted, and as I got older, I noticed those differences.

We had woodstoves to heat the house. For the cook stove, there was a gas tank in the backyard to provide fuel, which had to be filled by someone who brought the gas in a truck to our house. Since there was no grass in the front yard and very little in the backyard, we had much mud to manage when it rained. When it rained in the winter, our rain boots often seemed inadequate because the yard took so long to dry out. As soon as I was seven and could handle a garden hoe, I planted my mother's favorite flowers, zinnias, out front. Despite there being no grass, the zinnias made the place feel more like a home. They were all colors—pink, purple, and crimson. Their petals formed beautiful, bright frills. Although there were flowers in the front yard, there was garbage in the back. We had to pile trash there until the day came for burning it. I'm not sure how those days were determined, as they followed no clear pattern. But periodically, a burning day would come, and the trash pile would be set on fire. Some items, such as cans, refused to be burned and were left, scorched, for us to clear up. The debris left after the periodic fires was raked away as far from the house as possible.

Our little house in Moro, Arkansas, was very different from our old home near the black walnut grove. For one thing, there were no trees. Even though my whole family was together, there was something about the stark highway, the burning trash, and the mud that made a vague, nameless fear grow inside me. My family was trying to become acclimated to this new part of the state. But I began to feel that something awful would happen to us, although I wasn't sure what this would be. To combat this fear, I tried to figure out what I had to do to survive in this world that was so different from my beloved black walnut grove, but I didn't know what to do. There was not any real way to find out anything to make me feel better. So I began to practice silence. I learned to be quiet and to go about the day as if everything were fine. It wasn't.

As I said earlier, Highway 79 was busy, an endless rush of fast-driving cars and trucks. The drivers of these vehicles never thought of the people living in the isolated, rickety houses alongside the road. Their wheels ground on the asphalt, the drivers in a rush to get to wherever they were going. Many mornings, the highway was shrouded in a thick fog. When I was in first grade, one of my schoolmates was hit and killed by a car as she tried to cross the road to school. I can still see that little pile of her body lying on the side of the road underneath a dark blanket. I imagined what the moment of the car's impact felt like for her—the hot metal, the screeching tires. The thought of having to cross the road to get to school, even with my mother, became a frightening one. Every time we got to the edge of the road, I felt my heart pound faster. I was never comfortable having to cross, even though we lived in that house for several years and had the highway as a constant neighbor. When I was older and allowed to walk across the highway alone, the terribly thick fog made it so that I could not really determine if any cars were coming. I was always thankful to make it across without being hit. I never told anyone of my fear.

Illness was another source of fear for me. When I was seven, I contracted rheumatic fever. I had to spend the better part of the school year in bed. I hated to miss school. I liked seeing my friends. I liked learning, and staying home in bed was the last thing on earth that I wanted to do. Our school year followed the planting season, with a break in late spring and early summer that allowed us to work in the fields. Typically, during summers we were all expected to help tend to the cotton and the vegetable patches. Following my bout with rheumatic fever, I was not allowed to go to the field. That bothered me less than missing school, because I hated to be out in the sun all day. It was so hot, and the day began so early. My brother was not very happy about the fact that I was getting to stay home while they went to the field. He had no idea how much I wanted to be out of the house but instead had to stay in the house and mostly in the bed. I was just hoping that I could go back to school when it reopened after the summer break.

In spite of my being young, Mama trusted me with watching food that she left cooking, telling me when to turn off the burner. So this was one of the ways in which I could contribute to the family work even though I wasn't in the field. But my siblings, especially my brother, thought I was just getting away with not working. I think he didn't think I was really sick.

Later, during the next school year, when my older half sister took ill with the flu or at least a fever, no one ever told me what was really wrong with her. She had a very warm face, as I recall, and I surprised myself by the way I responded to her. I remember sitting beside her bed and keeping my hand on her face for the better part of a day. I was worried about her, and I wanted to do something to help her. I didn't know what to do. She slept the entire day, and that worried me as well. But whenever she woke up, I recall her saying that having my little hand on her face felt very good. I was glad I was helping her. I could've removed myself from the situation, hidden away from this frightening illness. Instead, I brought myself near and sat there, calm and full of love. This taught me something important about fear. I learned it couldn't always be avoided; it sometimes had to be faced.

There was a lot of concern about the weather in our house, especially whenever we thought a tornado might come. All dark clouds and threats of storms presented a cause for alarm. The clouds and blowing wind made me feel very small, as if I were cowering. If a thunderstorm came up at night, our parents would wake us and pull us out of bed. We were barely awake, but we had to put on our clothes because it was possible we'd have to leave the house. I had no idea where we were supposed to go. We had no car and there was no place to go. There was no shelter for us, and no plan. My parents were simply trying to manage their fears, but I didn't know that at the time, and it was very unsettling to have our parents get us up in the middle of the night to get dressed, only to go back to bed when the storm passed. I'm not sure how this behavior helped my parents manage their fear and sense of helplessness. It would have been better if we could have talked about storms and being afraid of them, but we didn't talk about them at all. Instead, we acted out of fear, without thinking or reflecting on our situation.

In 1955, I heard about the murder of Emmett Till. I was nine years old. I was frightened for my entire family and myself. In particular, when my brother was old enough to go away from home without us, I worried about his safety every minute of every day. I didn't really understand why Emmett Till was killed, but he was a boy and my brother was a boy and it seemed that things were more dangerous for boys. After all, I didn't hear of any girls being killed. Again, there was little conversation in my house about what had happened. My parents only told us we had to be careful. But I didn't know what I was supposed to be careful about. I knew I had to be cautious around white people, and that if I wasn't cautious, something bad could happen to me. But it seemed possible that anything I did could provoke violence from white people. If this was the case, how could I know what was safe to do, and what was dangerous? I continued to feel that the world was a dangerous place to be. But that danger felt unpredictable, and almost unknowable, so I had no idea what I was supposed to do about it.

Another source of fear for me was the story of my half brother, Garland. For as long as I could remember, my father had been talking about how Garland died because he was refused treatment at the local hospital. Daddy told that story at least once a week. Garland had complained for a few days about his stomach hurting. His complaints became more insistent as the days passed. My father and his wife gave him laxatives, hoping this would cause the trouble to pass, but the laxatives didn't help. A few more days passed, and he was in even more pain. Finally, Daddy took him to the Warner Brown Hospital in El Dorado, Arkansas. This hospital was for whites only, but my father was desperate, and I imagine that he hoped the staff might be willing to save Garland's life. After all, it was a hospital, and Daddy probably hoped they would be a little better than the average racist white person and keep the promise they made to help everyone regardless of their life circumstances. But he was wrong, and they refused to treat Garland. Instead, my father was instructed to take Garland to the charity hospital in Shreveport, Louisiana. That was seventy-five miles from where my family lived at the time.

Since there was no family car, my father had to arrange transportation, and it was not easy to do that. By the time they finally arrived at the hospital in Shreveport, too much time had passed. Garland had a ruptured appendix and died from the infection associated with it. My father never recovered from Garland's death, and his continual retelling of the story sank down into my gut. I was already worrying about storms and illness and being hit by a car on my way to school. I was grasping for words to describe these feelings, but no words came, and my family didn't provide them for me. No one around me seemed to have the language for the things that were crowding in on us, the way the mist rolled over the highway or the storms lowered down from the sky. Even my teachers, who taught me words for so many things, were not able to provide me with the consolation I so desperately needed. And I didn't have the language to ask the questions that were sitting inside me. So I just kept on gathering all the fearful and painful possibilities and burying them deep inside myself.

When I was eight years old and had been living in Moro for about three years, my youngest sister was born. I became a partial caretaker for her. It was good to have this new little person in our midst, and it was good for me to care for her. I took as much responsibility as a child can take in caring for a baby. I also did as much work as I could in the house to help my mother. When I rocked my baby sister or watered the zinnias, I could feel the fear subsiding. The routine—sweeping floors, carrying water—helped me to worry less about all the fearful things in my young life. It opened up a little space, and hope came into that space.

It was during this time that I began getting up before my family and sitting on the back steps to watch the sun rise. The quietness of the morning made me feel better. It was fun to see the little birds waking up as the sun rose. The warmth from it helped me to feel that things would be all right. I don't really know what caused me to wake up and consider opening a door to go sit outside. Something inside me just told me that, and I followed that voice.

I had a lot to think about. I wondered about so many things and didn't have anybody to talk to about them. I wondered if I could ask God for help—if God could maybe take away my fear. I couldn't tell, because I asked God for things and then did not get those things. I never had new shoes for the beginning of school and would miss the first few days of school because I had nothing to wear on my feet. I wondered why we couldn't order more pretty things from the catalogs. I saw that our handful of neighbors had so many things that we did not have. My classmates had nicer clothes than us, and when we were in stores, I saw many things that I liked. I was confused when I asked my parents for these things and was told that we just did not have money. We worked all the time, so I wondered why we didn't have money, but I didn't ask. I wondered a lot about God, and many of those mornings when I would get up early and go sit on the backdoor steps, observing the world as it was waking up, I wondered what it all had to do with us. I was too young to know how to really ask any questions about the ways we were treated. I did not really understand about racism; I just had an idea that things were not the way they needed to be and that I did not have to accept them—even though I had no idea what to do about anything. But something kept me turning to the sky, listening to the birds, and continuing to seek freedom in spite of it all. My mother's hope lived in me. My mother saying "Tomorrow is another day, and you don't know what it will bring" kept me willing to watch for the light of the new day.

2

A Bigger World

WHEN I WAS TWELVE YEARS OLD, my older sister moved to Grambling, Louisiana, about two hundred miles southwest of us, to take a teaching job. She needed a babysitter for her son, and my parents decided I should go stay with her for a couple of months to help out while I was off for my school's split term. I was under the impression I'd be staying with my sister for just a little while. Unfortunately, I was mistaken. The short term turned into the long term. My parents and sister decided I should stay and go to school in Grambling because they had a wonderful elementary school attached to Grambling College. The elementary school was considered a laboratory school partially because they trained teachers there. They had many resources, including a good library, art supplies, dance, and various extracurricular programs. I had no idea how to respond to the environment, the teachers, or my classmates.

My sixth-grade year in Grambling was a nightmare. My education in Arkansas had not prepared me to be a student in such a large school with so many more opportunities than I had ever seen in my first five years of school. I was not able to do the work that the students were doing because the level of instruction there was far more advanced than in my school back in Arkansas. The school was five times the size of my little Carver elementary school in Moro, and I stayed lost and behind my classmates for the entire year. One source of intense humiliation for me was a school musical. I was expected to participate because my class was involved. But the program included dance steps that I had never learned. I recall my teacher being very concerned that I couldn't learn those steps. I couldn't imagine what dance steps had to do with pushing my education forward. Even though the musical wasn't an academic pursuit, I burned with a sense of inadequacy. These feelings spilled over into my academic life in Grambling. Concerned about my lack of dancing skills, my teacher called my sister in for a conference and spoke to her about the possibility that I had a learning disability of some sort.

I had been a good student in Moro, making As and Bs in all my classes. Now my grades were Cs, Ds, and Fs. I was devastated by my low grades, but the teachers in Grambling thinking that I had learning deficits was even more traumatizing than my low grades. It damaged my ability to see myself as academically capable until I was out of college.

In addition to my academic woes, I had no friends in Grambling because my sister and her husband did not socialize with anyone who had children my age. So my sister put me in Girl Scouts in an effort to give me a chance to make friends away from school. This did not help because it was simply another challenge—like the musical, like school itself—that I did not feel prepared to tackle. At this point in my life, I didn't know how to meet new challenges with a resounding yes. Instead, I shrunk from these challenges, feeling small and inadequate. In Girl Scouts, we had overnight camping trips. I hated them; in the weeks leading up to each trip, I was anxious and full of dread. I didn't know how to start a fire or how to put up a tent. I had never seen a tent before, except in a catalog. Believe it or not, tents were a luxury—and one my family would've never considered. While I didn't know how to do any of the tasks, I did enjoy the food we made while camping. I learned how to make stew in a pot over an open fire, and I learned that graham crackers with toasted marshmallows and chocolate on them were quite delicious. I had never heard of s'mores before going to Grambling.

I was a chubby child and very self-conscious about it. My clothes were made by Mama from animal food sacks, and I thought my feet were too big because my family talked about my shoe size being hard to find. My hair was short and I wore it in little plaits, but I had seen photos of little Black girls with long hair and bangs, and I wanted to look more like them. Some of the girls in my class looked like that and had little adornments for their hair, along with ribbons. I wanted to have pretty things like that also. My family was much more inclined to buy necessities rather than hair ribbons and clips. We never had much money, and the money we did have was not spent on luxuries.

Because of all these factors, I felt ashamed of myself most of the time that I was in that school. Shame was my constant companion in Grambling, and fear followed me there as well. Before I began school, I stayed at my sister's house with her baby son. There were men—at least two men—staying in the back bedrooms of her fairly large house. I stayed in the front of the house with my nephew. My sister had made it clear that the guys had no business in that part of the house. I wonder if she sensed the danger in leaving a little girl alone in the house with these strange men.

One day the men made their way into the living room, where I was sitting with my little nephew. They came close, holding a stack of photos. One of them leaned toward me and held the photos right in front of my face. "Do you know what these are?" he asked. I looked at the pictures, revolted. I couldn't recognize what was happening in them. But I knew it made me feel deeply uncomfortable, like I wanted to run out of the room. I knew that the men had no business talking to me, and I had an idea that the photos were not wholesome. I also knew I should tell the men I didn't know what the photos depicted. I just wanted them to take their photos and go away. I wasn't sure how to make this happen, but I figured they would talk to me more if I told them I knew what the photos were depicting. "I have no idea," I said, hoping that would end the conversation. The photos were of people engaging in sex, and these guys were trying to find a way to become child molesters. I think the angels took care of me that day and made me say I did not know what the photos were.

"Don't ever tell your sister about this," they said before they left the room. I knew then that my instinct had been correct, and that it was important to trust my instincts. I wish my instincts could have made me more confident in myself and given me enough courage to tell the truth about the situation to my sister. Instead, I promised I would not tell, and I did not. So I continued my pattern of silently bearing up under circumstances that brought me great fear. This silence made me even more fearful, though. I was sure I would never be able to say anything about what was really going on in my head and heart. It would take me many years to learn how to tell the truth and learn that accurate naming and speaking the truth could bring freedom, not only to myself but to others as well.

I don't remember crying during that entire year in Grambling. Tears might have helped me to be less traumatized. Instead, I took all that trauma into my body and remained silent, having no way to process it. When I went back home,

I felt as if I had been gone a whole lifetime. Everything felt strange to me. Yet I was not able to process that strangeness. Instead, I worked all day in the fields, throughout the entire summer. I was constantly working and had no chance to rest or reflect on my experiences. I was a little child and had no way to make sense out of all that had happened to me and all the bad feelings that I had that year in Grambling about myself. Later I would get in touch with the rage I had toward my parents and my sister for putting me through that year of hell so she could have a free babysitter.

Though I had been gone for a year, my friends were still at Carver when we began seventh grade. They were glad to see me, and I felt so free and confident, as I was around people who weren't judging me for my hair or clothes. I was glad to be back in Arkansas, with my family and back in my school, away from the frightening strange men. Although there were many aspects of my life that felt out of my control, I decided to start exercising some agency when it came to my education. In Grambling, I'd felt disempowered in school. I was so far behind, it was impossible to even know where to begin in terms of improving my grades. So when I was back in Moro, I was motivated to do well. I knew what was going on, and I decided I had a chance to make good grades again. I was learning that even a small yes, in response to challenges, could result in newfound hope and confidence.

My efforts paid off. That year, my home economics teacher was fabulous. She helped me learn how to sew simple things such as dish towels, napkins, and even an apron. She also taught me to follow recipes to prepare a simple meal of things, such as mashed potatoes, green peas, and hamburger patties. After the end of seventh grade, at the beginning of summer, she came to my house to ask if I could work on a summer project, making food group charts. When I answered the door and saw my beloved teacher standing there,

I could barely believe my eyes. She told my mother, "I'm asking Catherine in particular because I can trust her to do the work." I was thrilled. This teacher whom I admired believed in me and chose me specifically. That was such a gift after my sixth-grade year and all its failures. In that moment, I was able to set aside the insecurities and fears of my past. I told my teacher yes with an open heart. My parents were proud to see that my teacher would come to the house to ask me to do something in the summer while we were out of school.

That would not be the last time an educational opportunity came to me unexpectedly. When I was in seventh and eighth grade, I wrote fictional short stories. My writing skills grew during this time. I was courageous enough to write a short story for the school newspaper that was actually published. I sat holding that newspaper in my hands when it was first given to me. It was hard to believe that the little girl who was scared to open her mouth two years before had written and published a short story in the school paper. The story was called "The Twins' Mother," and it was about a woman finding a cure for cancer. My friends liked it and were surprised I had written it. After lacking words to describe my own experiences, I was able to put words into fiction in ways that completely surprised me. It amazed me to think of others reading these words. Perhaps I could help them understand their own experiences as well. I also grew in my drawing abilities. I enjoyed drawing simple pictures of internal organs such as lungs, hearts, and kidneys for class assignments in biology. It was fun to look at something and be able to reproduce it.

During seventh and eighth grade, it was good to watch myself work and to see that I was capable of staying with a task and completing it without having to have an adult standing over me to make sure I followed through. These new experiences helped me to look forward to high school.

A few times I allowed myself to think that I might go to college when I finished high school. But the judgment of the teachers in Grambling stayed with me, even during these successes. They thought I had learning deficits. Sometimes those words came back to me, dragging me down and making me afraid for my future. It would take me many years—many hours of psychotherapy and inner exploration—to overcome what was set in motion during that one year in Grambling.

3

Desperation Burned Down
Our House

IN 1960, WHEN I WAS FOURTEEN, the man for whom Daddy was a sharecropper moved into a new house he had built, and we were allowed to move into his old house in Moro. I had never lived in a painted house, and it was my most cherished daydream to live in a house painted white and with lots of flowers in the yard. This house was white. Not only was it white; there were also seven beautiful weeping willow trees out front. And there was grass growing. After years of living in dirt and mud, this felt like a luxury. There were flowers whose names I did not know then. Later in life, I would see these flowers, know their names, and realize I had seen them before in that yard. The front yard was large and long, which made it easy for us to ride our bike. We had one bike that my sister, brother, and I shared. It was wonderful to be in that house. I realized that I had longed to live in a white house for a long time, and I was so glad that we had this place. It was quite nice inside too. After all, it was the house that the landowner had lived in before he became rich enough to build a bigger and better house. Of course, it was our labor that was making him richer. But I was not thinking about all that at the time. I enjoyed the house.

The house had no indoor plumbing, but it was very nice otherwise, with two rooms serving as a living room and a kitchen. Then there was a long room that did not have a partition, which we used as our bedrooms. My parents were at one end, and my two siblings slept at the other end. During the winter months, there were many bushel baskets of sweet potatoes stored along the wall of that long bedroom. We covered the baskets with blankets so that they were not visible. Needless to say, we ate sweet potatoes every day. I am amazed at how much I still like them, considering how many there were to eat in my early life.

I slept on the couch in the front room, which could be converted into a small bed by letting the back and front down. I was really glad to have that space to myself. I could stay up and sneak reading until my parents discovered my small flashlight and made me go to sleep. Ever since I first read books on my father's lap, I loved to read. It was my link to a world I could not even imagine, in spite of my great imaginative skills. The books I read helped me escape to places I had never heard of before, opening up the world to me in a way that created space that I did not have to share. Books allowed me to dream of more than the small world of Moro, Arkansas.

I was not daunted by the lack of indoor plumbing or any other challenges around being in this house. Instead, I saw every aspect of this house as a sign of hope. I enjoyed picking wildflowers and placing them around the house. The weeping willows were beautiful. I enjoyed sitting under them, though I was vigilantly on the lookout for the little green frogs who seemed to love the trees as much as I did. They were playful and harmless, but I did not like them because they were much too fast in hopping from one place to another without giving me any prior notice of their intention.

As I had done in our old house, I woke up early, before the other members of my family, and sat outside waiting for the sun to rise. This was the best house I had ever lived in, and I was thrilled. I worked in the yard because I loved the flowers. I did a lot of housework because I was proud of that house. After all, it was painted white. Our house sat on the edge of the farm that Daddy was charged with working, and that made it easy for us to get to the field work each day. While working in the field was not my favorite thing to do, I developed the habit of simply doing what I had to do each day.

I have said many times that sharecropping was simply glorified slavery. Whether it came with a house, white or any other color, does not matter.

I watched my father year after year begin the farm year with hope. He hoped he could end the farm season with money enough to pay his part of the costs related to the crop production. And he hoped to have money left over to get necessities for us. He also hoped, every year, to have a decent Christmas. He spoke often about this hope. He would talk about taking us to town to shop after the settlement with the landowner was finished. But each year was just the same as the one before. When he paid everything he had to pay to the landowner, he had nothing. There was no money to take us shopping. A few times we would go to the Dairy Queen and each of us got a pint of ice cream, which was all Daddy could afford to spend after he settled the bills from the previous year. Then he had to begin again by going into debt with the landowner. The cycle was not ever going to be broken because the system was functioning exactly as it was designed to, to make sure the landowner got richer and the sharecropper stayed poor or got poorer.

I was living in my little teenage world of exhilaration because we were finally living in this white house, which was somehow an affirmation to me that our economic life was getting better. However, quite the contrary was true. Nothing had changed and my father knew it, and he had no reason to believe it was ever going to change. How does an illiterate African American man find the path to hope that he can finally make enough money to provide for his family and have a little bit of economic freedom? What path would lead to such a new place? My father did not see any such path for himself and us. He lived in utter desperation and the deep despair it generates. While I was living in a house of hope, my father was living in that house of desperation. I could sense this, but I didn't have any words for it. I had trouble finding those words because my family never had any conversations about the desperation that surrounded us.

We didn't talk about religion in our house. Mama took us to church and Daddy stayed at home. But every Sunday morning, Daddy would get up singing spirituals. His favorite one was "Father, I stretch my arms to thee, no other help I know." He could sing fairly well, and I can hear him singing as I write these words. I never thought of Daddy as having much faith because he never talked about God nor prayed out loud around us, but every day he walked a six-acre farm to see what had transpired the night before with the crop. He sang that same spiritual over and over, along with a few others that I don't really recall. He had hope that one year things would change and he would not be just a poverty-stricken Black man who had to take his little girl with him to write his name. He knew his life was supposed to be about more than that. He passed that dream on to us, even though he was not able to realize it himself.

I wonder how Daddy managed to keep planting a crop every year and hoping that the next year would be the one that produced such a huge yield that he would actually find he had some cash coming to him when the bills were paid. The sharecropping system made it impossible for sharecroppers to realize that type of result. It was rigged such that the costs for the year equaled all the money the sharecropper had earned. In spite of being up against this reality, my father called on God. I wonder what he thought of that God who never seemed to be responsive to him. Nothing changed in the outer world, and I have no real way to know what changed in his inner world.

These days I wonder what my father thought about the white house and the fact that the landowner's opportunity to build it was directly related to my father's and our labor and the yearly crops we harvested. He must have wondered where God was in this white house that I was so happy to be living in. I think my father saw the control and exploitation in the situation far better than I did, and he began to assume that God was not going to rescue him.

Since my father did not talk about his desperation or intentions, I have to imagine that he decided he had to do something because, though he sang "no other help I know" but God's, there seemed to be no help. He decided to take matters into his own hands. He came up with a remedy. But desperation usually gives birth to remedies that fall short.

I learned that my father was taking out an insurance policy on the house. The policy was for fifteen hundred dollars, and I wondered why he was doing this. But I didn't think too much about it. We had many severe thunderstorms and windstorms that came close to becoming tornadoes, so I thought he might believe that the house would get destroyed by one of those storms and we could collect the insurance.

I was wrong. Though my parents didn't tell us much about their business, they decided I had to be told of the scheme that Daddy had devised. I wish I had not been told. It made me very angry and sad. I thought of the flowers and the weeping willows, thought of the white paint peeling off in the fire that my father was planning set to the house.

On the day Daddy put his plan into action, in May 1962, we packed all that we could in our old gray Pontiac late one night. We all got in the car and waited for Daddy. He finally came out. As we drove down the long driveway, I could feel tears in my eyes, but I did not turn my head to look back at the house that I cherished and would never see again. I wondered to myself whether the little tree frogs would withstand the fire. I wondered whether there would be another place in the world for me, now that the little white house was being reduced to ashes. I wondered where God was. If my father felt God was the only help he knew, then my father's desperate action proved that God's help did not come soon enough. I wondered how much one should depend on God anyway.

My father's desperation only created more desperation in our lives. Fifteen hundred dollars was so little money, even more than fifty years ago. It was gone in a blink of the eye. It did not make our overall situation any better. It actually made everything worse. We became homeless for a short while. It was not easy to find another place to live. It was too late in the farming season to get another sharecropping assignment. So we spent the summer living in a shabby, unpainted house with sparse furnishings and no summer garden. Because we had no farm work, we had no income in the fall. As was always the case before this, each member of my family suffered separately, in silence. I could sense the fears my parents had about our future, but those fears were never named. I realized the dream of our own house was just that—a dream. The house had never been ours to begin with. Still, it seemed at the time that the white man's white house was the closest thing my family would ever have to a home. It would be years before I would claim the dream of a home for myself. Even then, I would sometimes think of my father—the dreams I'm sure he had, and the way he was born into a system set up to crush those dreams. Desperation was the only way of life he knew, and his attempts to alleviate that desperation only drove us into more desperate circumstances. It seemed there was no way out. I did not know then that the system of white supremacy—and the sharecropping system, slavery by a different name—were designed to trap people like my father in this cycle of desperation. And it was in naming this that I would begin to have hope for a different way to be.

My parents tried to rely on other work as a way out of our desperate financial situation. My cruel and vindictive uncle, my mother's brother, was the principal of George Washington Carver School. He had the power to hire and fire whomever he chose. My uncle was the most dishonorable person I had ever met. He would take things from the school. He ate at our house but never brought a gift of any type or did anything to help my family, though he knew we were poor. The summer after our house burned down, my uncle ran a summer program that allowed him to give jobs to teenagers, but he refused to hire me, while hiring my classmates whose families were quite well off. He knew we needed the money. These are just a few examples of his lack of regard for his own sister and her family.

In addition to working as a sharecropper, my father worked at George Washington Carver School as a part-time janitor in the wintertime before the farming season began. My mother worked there as a teacher. My uncle knew about my father's arson for insurance money and, acting in a morally superior manner, chose to fire both him and my mother because of it. When he fired my parents, he left them with no way to provide for us. All income to our family was lost. In years before that, particularly when school was out for the summer and his wife was away visiting her family, my uncle had been a regular guest for dinners. The summer after he fired my parents, he never came to our house. Perhaps he was ashamed of his behavior, or maybe he just knew we would barely have any meals. That was the only year in my early life that I recall being afraid that we would not have food.

As I was growing up, we had a wonderful vegetable garden every summer. Although we were poor, we always had plenty of tomatoes, cucumbers, okra, lettuce, peas, potatoes, greens, and peaches that we bought from the processing plant because they were not very expensive. Mama always canned peaches and other fruits and vegetables so that we'd have the canned items to eat over the winter. But this summer was different. I remember that Mama slept a lot. I understand that she was dealing with her sense of immobilization and helplessness. She had always believed that one could find a reason to have hope no matter what was happening. But she didn't know what to do about this situation because there was no place to get a job in our little rural town. In the past Mama had always said, "Tomorrow is another day, and you never know what will come." She held on to that idea all summer. She got a teaching job in the fall in a little town near us, which was a surprising blessing.

My father never talked about what happened. He was quieter than ever. He was in the house all the time since he was not farming. He began being sick a lot. He was old enough to qualify for social security but had never had enough of any type of work, or income, to collect it. We spent time going back and forth to doctors and to Social Security offices trying to get help.

The insurance money didn't last long, so we had to figure out what to do for food. In the end, we turned to what were called "commodities"—government-issued food. Cheese, canned meat, dry milk, rice, peanut butter, yellow cornmeal, flour, and a few other nonperishables were given to us during that summer. Mama made all kinds of interesting things with them, as she always could do with meager

resources. Old neighbors from the neighborhood on Highway 79 gave us vegetables. We made it through the summer.
Mama began teaching at her new job. We started school.

My father had a stroke in November 1962 and died. I was
devastated. First the trauma of losing the house I loved.
Now I had lost my Daddy, whom I loved also, though I am
not sure I would have been able to say that at the time. I was
so confused about everything. I was scared. I felt as if the
earth had moved and I was walking on quicksand all the
time. My world was torn into pieces and I simply kept picking up the pieces trying to figure out how to make them fit
back together. They refused to fit.

As far as I know, my parents were law-abiding citizens up
until this moment of breaking the law as they were caught
by desperation. Desperation's voice is unreliable. It causes
one to lose sight of many things, such as the long-term impact of one's actions on everyone involved. My father's desperation was understandable. He lived in a racist town, and
sharecropping would have trapped him for the rest of his life.
Even his brother-in-law was not on his side. Like my father,
I have at times faced limited options and had societal factors
stacked up against me. And even though I've never gotten to
the point where I've felt I had to act in as desperate a manner
as Daddy did, I have made unfortunate choices at times because of my sense of desperation and lack of faith that things
could or would change. I have taken years to learn how to
trust myself and how to ask for help from others in my community. These qualities have helped me to better hear the
voice of discernment, which has led me to better places than
my father was led.

He had no community that was trying to support him.
He was up against perennial hardship with no hope of the
tide ever turning. He had no way to imagine anything but
defeat until his dying day. Unlike my father, I had an edu-

cation and the possibility of even more education, which was always considered to be the ticket out of poverty and constant hardship. Though that may not be totally true, my education has helped me in one way or another to have options. One other difference between my father and me is that I was able to get good psychological counseling that helped me to gain a greater sense of agency than I had when entering college. My father had no way to achieve this sense of agency, even though he often proclaimed he could "cover the ground that he stood on." I'm not sure he always believed that to be true.

Confronting one's self helps to clarify weaknesses and strengths, which then enables new ways of seeing that are necessary to facing the struggles of life that lead to desperation. Desperation cannot be allowed to erase hope. Desperation has to be named and help has to be sought before hope becomes a constant refrain in the heart of a person. Isolation is the greatest supporter of desperation. My father had isolation heaped upon him. I understand now a little better what it must have been like for him. He loved us. He wanted our lives to be better.

4

Escape from Arkansas

FOLLOWING MY FATHER'S DEATH IN 1963, we moved from Moro to Brinkley, a city with a population of over four thousand. For us, this was a move to "the city." In comparison with the towns we'd lived in before, paved roads and streetlights were impressive. My mother got a job teaching at Wheatley Elementary School. This school was about ten miles from Brinkley, so she had to drive there each day and drop us off at school earlier than usual because of her schedule. By this time, my brother and I were in high school. I knew how to drive but had nothing to drive since we had only one car. We were relieved when Mama worked out alternate transportation for herself and I was able to drive us to school.

The uncle who had fired my parents found us a house, just a few months after the firing. His help always fell short of being all that it seemed to be at first glance. The house was dismal. My uncle had led us to believe that it would have inside plumbing. However, it didn't take us long to learn that the toilet was not connected to a sewer system and that raw sewage was going underneath the house. This was a distress-

ing way to live, but because we were poor, we had few other
options for homes.

By this time, at age seventeen, I had become a full-blown
parental child. I felt responsible for my family. I helped
Mama with cleaning, cooking, and washing everyone's
clothes on the weekend. I got a job at a local hotel as a short-
order cook. I was terrible at it, but I managed to keep the
job during the summer. I was always looking out for us and
trying to find things that would help us. My father's death
left me with a sense of vulnerability. I realized how quickly
we could slide into that desperation. Because of this, I was
motivated to make a better future for my mother and siblings. One day at school, I heard about a homeowner who
needed to find a renter for a new house she was building.
She was the mother of one of my favorite teachers. I was too
shy to speak to the woman directly, but I spoke to my teacher
about it. We urgently needed to move from the wreck of a
house we were living in at the time—the one with the sewage
problem. Although I had trouble speaking up to advocate for
myself, I found my voice when I had to speak for my family.
I surprised myself, reaching into my being for a strong voice.
I was also surprised by my ability to identify something I
wanted and then manifest it as a reality.

I went home that day from school and told Mama I had
found a way for us to move into a better house. She was very
interested in pursuing the possibility. It was 1963; the rent for
a two-bedroom house in Brinkley was twenty-five dollars a
month. The next day I told my teacher that we wanted to rent
the house. He told me to tell his mother, who was a teacher in
the elementary school. I went over to the elementary school
and found her. My heart was beating in my throat when I
introduced myself. She didn't know who I was, and I had
only the connection to my teacher, her son, to recommend
me. I filled my lungs with air and asked her if my family

could rent the house. I promised her we would pay the rent regularly and take great care of the property. She smiled at me. "I would be happy to rent to your family," she said. "I'm thrilled to have the place rented out."

I could barely believe that we were moving into this brand-new house. It was white, like the house that had burned down in Moro. We didn't have pretty flowers and weeping willow trees, but it didn't matter because the house was new and had indoor plumbing. I was so happy, and I worked even harder to help with all the chores. I did so much that my siblings had hardly any chores to do. I cooked, cleaned, and washed and ironed all our clothes on the weekend. For the first time, I felt I had some control of my future. This motivated me to take even more control of our home life and surroundings.

While Mama was teaching classes, she was also *taking* classes. She was going to college through correspondence, as well as attending on-site classes in a nearby town. Mama graduated from college in the summer of 1964. I graduated from high school that year.

Our relocation to Brinkley was good for all of us. We settled into our life without Daddy as best we could. We managed to carry our grief, mostly by ourselves, because we kept up our tradition of suffering in silence. We talked about Daddy sometimes. But we didn't talk about our grief. It seemed impossible to put words to it. Instead, we managed it.

One day, I heard a broadcast on the radio. It was from the Church of Christ in Memphis. I began listening to them on a regular basis and decided they would be a good group to be connected with. However, the only Church of Christ congregation in our town was white. I decided to write to the Memphis Church of Christ and ask them to come to Brinkley and baptize me, as well as my sister and my brother.

They obliged. The irony is that while the white congregation in Brinkley was glad for us to be baptized in their church, they wouldn't invite us to attend, and they never made any inquiries about us or our well-being. I wonder now if they drained the pool after we were baptized. What disingenuous people they all were, for initially engaging in the charade of being concerned about us. Neither the folks from Memphis nor the local folks cared about me or my family. They were playing roles, and we were merely characters in their story. If I had it to do again, I would not. I wanted to know more about God and I was seeking help. I needed a counselor but didn't have any way of finding one. Jesus—the Jesus I had met in the Children's Bible Stories series I read when I was younger—was important to me. I wanted to know more about him but didn't know how I could do that. I thought the Church of Christ folks would help. They didn't. They were probably patting themselves on the backs for baptizing us, but our ongoing welfare was too much trouble for them to be concerned about.

Mama was angry with me about getting baptized in the Church of Christ. She wanted me to stay in our Baptist denomination. It must have felt like betrayal to have your teenage children joining another religious denomination, especially one that was egotistical enough to declare itself the only true church. One day, I overheard my aunt telling Mama that I was going to kill her as I had my father. Mama didn't deny it, and at that time I wasn't sure why she didn't tell the truth and stand up for me. She knew I didn't cause my daddy's death. As I think about it now, I understand. But this accusation by my aunt was painful to hear especially because she was my favorite aunt whom I had loved for as long as I could remember. I wondered whether anyone noticed how much I had been trying to do for my family. However, I just went on my way as I always did with trauma. I didn't know what else to do. Whom could I speak to, and what could I say?

My two years at Marian Anderson High School in Brinkley, the school for Black students, were generally good. I ran for Miss Marian Anderson even though chubby, short-haired, dark girls were not supposed to be homecoming queen. The contest was based on how much money the girls could raise. I had some ideas for making money that other girls didn't consider. By this time, I was used to finding ways to support myself. I used this skill in the homecoming queen competition. I sold sandwiches to the field workers with whom I spent several days. I asked friends and family to support me. I had a few bake sales and raffled a couple of items. In the end, I came in second place to my math teacher's sister. She had more resources than I did, including long straight hair and much lighter skin. Everyone thought she was the person who looked like a homecoming queen. Colorism—prejudice against darker-skinned people, even within the Black community—has always been an issue in my life. There have been times when I was told I was "pretty for such a dark-skinned girl." My own aunt talked about how ugly I was as a baby to my face. Colorism surely impacted my chances in the Miss Marian Anderson contest.

A few weeks after that contest, my math teacher, who was the sponsor for the school yearbook, asked if I would be editor in chief of the Marian Anderson Yearbook. I was floored. He told me he watched the way I worked when I was running for homecoming queen and was quite impressed. He even told me his sister had won because she had a lot of folks give large sums of money to her. I could barely believe I was being asked to do such an important job. I was very pleased about it. My math teacher had faith in me; the question was whether I could say yes and have the same faith in myself. Up to this point, I'd had so few opportunities to say yes. I did not hesitate, and I liked the way saying yes made me feel.

A major part of the job for the yearbook editor was selling ads. I did this quite successfully, and we put together a very good yearbook. The yearbook was published in my senior year, and my position on its editorial team was vindication for me. I did find that it alienated me even further from the young men in my school. My brother ended up taking me to the senior prom, but it was worth it to me. I preferred success to attention from young men with tiny egos who could not allow a girl to be smart or successful.

After I graduated from high school, I wondered what was next for me. An opportunity came in the form of my half brothers and sisters. My father's first wife, with whom he had seven children, had passed away several years before he met and married my mother. Some of my half brothers and sisters were almost as old as my mother. Several of them lived far from Arkansas, in Los Angeles. After I graduated from high school, I moved to Los Angeles to live with my youngest half brother and go to college. I thought everything would be better there than they were in Arkansas. I was expecting magic, but that new place had many lessons in store for me.

I declared I would never come back to the South. I thought I was done with small-town racist oppression and small-minded thinking on the part of Black people. I had no idea that racism was alive and well all over the country.

I worked it out with my brother to send me money for a bus ticket, which he was glad to do. Mama agreed I could attend college in Los Angeles. She could see it was an opportunity unlike any she'd ever had. I was so thankful. I had to get out of Arkansas. I needed to have a chance to explore my head and heart in better ways. I needed to be free of feeling responsible for my family and of working so hard to help make everything good for everyone. I was not able to articulate this at the time. It would be many years before I was able to understand how difficult it was to be a parental child, absorbing the responsibilities that emerged from my father's death. I couldn't give language to the voice that was telling me to leave Arkansas. I only heard the internal mandate to go. Even at this age, I was beginning to practice discernment about my life. However, I didn't always understand what was behind my ability to make complicated decisions, what made me know how to say yes. While I couldn't articulate this sense of discernment, I also didn't question it.

I had never ridden a Greyhound bus for more than a couple of hours. So the trip to Los Angeles, which took two nights and almost three days, was beyond anything I could have imagined. On a Greyhound, the first day is not too bad. You look out the window, eager to see the changing land-scape, and are excited about the adventure. But the second day, the fatigue of being on a bus begins to set in. By the time you sleep a second night on the bus, it begins to feel as if you can't stand it for another minute. But you still have the better part of another day before arriving at your destination. It had been the longest three days of my life, it seemed, by the time I arrived in Compton, California.

I was so glad to be out of Arkansas. It was strange being in a big city and being away from home for the first time as an eighteen-year-old. No one had talked to me about apply-ing to colleges or possibly going to a four-year school. My mother's and half brother's assumption was that I would go to a two-year school. There was not really any discussion about any other choices. The thought was that the two-year college would be free, but that turned out not to be true. I was not considered a resident of California, so I had to pay $180 for the first term. I didn't know I would have to pay that much. I had been told it was $8.50, but that was the tuition for residents. So we had to quickly hustle up the money. It came from Mama and my half brother. My half brother was always generous and was always supportive and affirming of me and all I tried to do. He continued to be a positive force in my life until his death many years later.

My first year of college was an adjustment from high school in Brinkley. Compton College had large classrooms, and some of my classes had more students than had been in my entire high school. My high school graduating class had less than thirty people. My college history class had two hundred or more.

Some classes were more challenging than others. I thrived in my speech class. My speech professor sent me to speak to the forensics coach about joining the college forensics team. I had no idea that this type of thing existed, and it was great to go the tournaments and compete in several categories. I did impromptu, oral interpretation, and debate. My coach was great. He was affirming and thought of me as a person who did good work.

I went with the team to UCLA, USC, Long Beach State, UC Redlands, and many other places I had never known existed. It was challenging to speak under pressure and to debate with students whose high school education had been so much stronger than mine. But I was determined to succeed and did well because I was much smarter than I thought I was, and I worked hard. I didn't win prizes, but my self-confidence grew by leaps and bounds. It was good for me to discover that I could walk into an impromptu round where I would be given a topic and could put together a decent speech in a few minutes. I was amazed about this because even though I had a fairly strong voice in high school, we didn't have public speaking classes.

I was not as successful in all my classes. I had a very hard time in one English class. I didn't like the teacher. She seemed starched and ironed and was unapproachable. She seemed oblivious to my presence in her class. We read *Billy Budd* and a lot of other novels I had never heard about in my life. I didn't understand what they were really about. I made a D in that class.

Second semester, I discovered philosophy and a professor I enjoyed.

Along with that, I took a world literature class and really thrived on Russian authors. Turgenev was my favorite. While my typing was atrocious, my professor thought I had great ideas and good-quality analysis. I made an A that term in English. Since this was part two of the class I had almost failed, the grades were combined and I ended up having a B when it was all calculated.

All my teachers were white. Unlike many of my class-mates, I had never had a white teacher before. Some of these teachers were more hospitable than others. I was deeply af-fected by their energy. It was clear that some of them were able to see me as a person and others were not. When a teacher was able to see me as a person, I thrived. When they were unable to see me as a person, I had a harder time in their class. I didn't realize how important relationship is for teachers to have with students, in terms of creating an en-vironment where the student feels that the teacher is inter-ested in their success and is willing to show that interest.

Although I was in a new environment, the old habit of suf-fering in silence had followed me from Arkansas to Los Ange-les. It is difficult, when growing up with so much trauma and silence, to learn new practices. I don't really know how I nav-igated that first year. I was sad and lonely. There were times when I was on the verge of being suicidal. There was too much unfamiliar territory in my life. I didn't like living with my brother. My classes for the most part were too large, and I felt intimidated. And there was no one to talk to about it. At least, that's what I thought. In reality, there were mental health resources, but I didn't know about such things. The habit of bearing all my burdens alone and in silence continued. It was a sad time. My academic success was a gift, considering the weight my soul was bearing during that time. Toward the end of the school year, I finally learned about the college counseling center. I sought help from them, only to learn that there was a wait list. It was difficult to realize that help was available but not immediately. It created a sense of hope and a simultaneous feeling of hopelessness. Still, I placed myself on the list. But a slot didn't open up for me until I was back in Arkansas for the summer. Of course, I couldn't take advantage of this, since I wasn't in Los Angeles.

That summer, the Watts Revolt occurred. On August 11, 1965, a young African American man was pulled over by police for drunken driving, and a physical confrontation ensued. Over the next five days, civil unrest broke out throughout the Watts neighborhood in southern Los Angeles in response to allegations of police abuse. My mother and I watched it on the news. We saw billowing smoke and police training their guns on citizens. My mother wasn't sure that she would let me go back to California. The news reports made it appear as if the city was being burned down. It was not. But we couldn't prove that by watching the news. I was worried, even though I knew the violence was not in Compton. This was one more thing to worry about, on top of finding money for school and my grades and my family. I wondered what I could do. I felt powerless, but I also knew I had made it all the way to Los Angeles once, and that therefore I did have some control over my life. Still, I had to tuck away all my concerns about what was going on in Watts. I wanted to go back to Los Angeles, so I did everything I could to get my mother to believe it was safe for me to return to school.

While I was in Arkansas that summer, I had to find a job. If I didn't make money, I wouldn't be able to return to Los

Angeles. So I babysat for someone in the morning and looked after the baby's incapacitated grandfather at the same time. Then I spent an hour walking to my next job as a short-order cook at the hotel, arriving each day by 3:00 p.m. and working until 11:00 p.m. So each day I worked from 7:30 a.m. until 11:00 p.m. I was paid $25 a week for the babysitting/eldercare job and $3.03 a day for the cooking job. I worked six days at the hotel and made $18.18 a week. I'm not sure why we were paid the three cents. I allowed myself to spend only eighteen cents each week. I saved every penny because I wanted to get my own apartment when I went back to California in the fall. It was a miserable summer, but I was determined to get back to California and to have enough money to get an apartment. I felt like I was on a heroine's journey and I had to be disciplined and stay focused.

As I prepared for the fall, I bought cheap little household goods such as a can opener, spatulas, and glasses. I couldn't afford much, but I wanted small, practical things that would go in an apartment. By the end of summer, I had saved enough money to get an apartment with one of my former classmates from Arkansas who was also attending college in Compton. Back in California, we got a place for seventy-five dollars a month. It was partially furnished. We both got jobs working at the same barbecue restaurant. Although we were young, we were smart and willing to work hard, which we did. The barbecue place was open until 2:00 a.m., and we didn't have a car. We had to hustle rides from others who worked there, and we paid them to drop us home. The buses didn't run that late.

We were in school and working. Finally, we found better jobs working downtown in a dress shop company's offices. The work wasn't complicated, but it was eight hours a day, so we had to take classes at night. Again, there was a problem regarding transportation. In Los Angeles, transportation was always a challenge. I had to work to afford a car, but I needed a car in order to get to work. Many job opportunities were far away from my apartment. Before I got a car, I got stranded at school one evening and couldn't get home. A friend had offered me a ride, but her car broke down not long after we left campus. We ended up having to walk for about three hours to get to our respective homes. Things like that were constantly happening to me, as I was broke and reliant on whatever transportation I could manage to organize. Though it took a while, I did finally manage to get an old car. It wasn't in the best shape, but I came to be used to having old cars until long after graduating from college, I finally bought my first new car. The old cars that I managed to own got me to school, to work, and around in the city.

I was learning how to live on my own, but I still had much to learn about discernment. In college, I became friendly with a group of young men. One of these young men was especially attracted to me and I to him. He was on the Compton College soccer team and was from Jamaica. He was fascinating to me. I was not used to dating. Most of the boys in high school had not liked me since I was always doing the jobs that no girl had done before, such as yearbook editor or running for student council president. So having this handsome young man find me attractive was a bit intoxicating for a brief moment.

It didn't take me long to learn that he was violent and exploitative. As is often the case with people in abusive situations, I tried to talk myself into believing he was better than he was. However, I could no longer make excuses for him after he hit me during an argument in my apartment one night. I went to tend to my eye, which was beginning to bruise and swell, hoping he would be gone by the time I got an icepack. He was—but so was all the money in my wallet.

I called my brother and explained the situation to him. At the time, I didn't have the strength to end the relationship with my abuser, and I wanted my brother's support. My brother gave me the best gift a family member can give to someone who is not smart enough to separate themselves from a violent and exploitative person. "You need to listen carefully and believe me," he said. "This is the first and last time that you are to call me after a man has been abusive to you." He said this not because he was unsympathetic but because he would not tolerate abuse and did not want me to tolerate it either. It was a good gift and a good word. I never needed to call my brother about such a situation again, because after that I stayed away from violent men. At that time, I still didn't know how to fully see and value myself. My brother was able to see me and value me, though, and eventually this taught me how to do the same for myself. A few days later, the former abuser came to my apartment and tried to reconcile with me. I am certain he thought he could continue to take advantage of me. I simply stood my ground, remembering what my brother had told me. The abuser finally came to realize that I meant it when I said I was in fact done with him. I will always be grateful to my brother for being so clear and matter-of-fact about not becoming a collaborator with me in letting myself be captivated by a man who would wish to harm me. This taught me to be more discerning about the men I let into my life.

My brother made another significant impact on my life. A few months after the situation with the abusive man, I began to feel extremely tired all the time. At first, I thought I was just working too much, but it got progressively worse. So I finally went to the doctor. After several visits and many tests, I was diagnosed with hyperthyroidism, a condition in which the thyroid is producing too much thyroid hormone. This had to be corrected by surgery. I was a young woman in college, with no health insurance and very little money, and now I needed surgery. Thankfully, my brother had a good friend who was a general surgeon. My brother connected me with him. I went to see this doctor, and he scheduled me for surgery. I'm not sure how I managed to have surgery without having insurance, since it is difficult to even get past the front desk these days without it. But I did.

My surgery was a success. As a result of meeting my surgeon, Dr. Ross M. Miller Jr., an entire world opened up for me. Dr. Miller was an amazing person. He had graduated from college and medical school early and decided to become a general surgeon. By the time I met him, he had been in practice for quite a while. His office was in the Charles R. Drew Medical Complex. It was amazing for me to have a Black physician, but now I discovered an entire group of Black physicians and a Black pharmacist who owned a drugstore.

During one of my follow-up visits, Dr. Miller indicated that he needed a receptionist. He wanted to hire someone to begin immediately. In fact, he was desperate to find someone. I was tired of my dress shop office job, so I applied and was hired almost instantly. I had never worked in a doctor's office. I had no idea what I needed to do. But I knew I could learn, and I didn't mind working hard. Dr. Miller needed someone to be there to answer the phone and to let his patients in at 2:00 p.m., since that was when he arrived there after surgery each day. I was so glad to have a better work situation, but I was really nervous on my first few days. There was far more to learn than at my previous job. But Dr. Miller could see that I would work hard and learn quickly. He also could see that school was incredibly important to me, and he made it clear that he was interested in my school success also and wanted to support me in whatever way he could. I would be able to go to school in the daytime again. He let me know I needed to be there when he was—from 2:00 to 6:00 p.m. on Mondays, Tuesdays, Thursdays, and Fridays and from 9:00 a.m. to 1:00 p.m. on Saturdays. I couldn't believe my ears. I would have all day Wednesdays to do schoolwork, and I would be home at night. I could attend class in the mornings without having to worry about commuting home in the dark every night. It was too wonderful to be true. I was still learning how to use my voice, but one of the first lessons I'd learned was how to say yes—especially to opportunities like this one.

Dr. Miller was one of the first people to invest in my education. He made sure I understood the importance of finishing college, and his generosity in terms of my work schedule spoke volumes to me. I didn't really know how to take in his goodness, but I thought the best way I could say thank you was by simply doing well in school and being an excellent office assistant. I managed to do both. In the office, I learned how to write accident reports to insurance companies and lawyers for people who were in accidents. I also learned how to bill insurances for surgeries, how to bill Medicaid, and how to bill patients for balances after all insurance reimbursements were made. Along with this, I had to learn how to do basic things in the office, such as sterilizing instruments and keeping the hot packs used for physiotherapy up to par. I learned fast and I did a good job. It took me more than a few years to realize the gift that Dr. Miller was for me. At the time, I didn't think of him as teacher or mentor. I thought of him first as the surgeon who performed my subtotal thyroidectomy when I was twenty years old, then as my employer. I worked for him until I graduated from college and moved to Georgia. With his help, it was easier to get through my undergraduate work. If I had to work in the food industry or some other place with a more strictly regimented schedule, I would have struggled significantly.

Soon after going to work for Dr. Miller, I transferred to George Pepperdine College, which was located in Los Angeles at the time, close to USC.

Having a new environment was good for me. The school was small and a break from the big classes at Compton College, which I had never liked. It was exciting to be going to a school I had researched and was happy to attend. It gave me a sense of agency unlike any I'd experienced in my life so far.

Having a car also gave me a sense of agency. I had an old 1960s Ford Falcon that I bought for very little money. It was fine for getting me to school, work, and the grocery store. The car made it possible for me to work for my half sister, who lived nearby, on Wednesdays, my day off. I was able to help her and others who didn't have transportation. My car ownership also made it possible for me to go to events that I would have missed otherwise. For example, I learned about events where political dignitaries were speaking, which I would have never heard about if I had not been working for Dr. Miller, who, in addition to being a doctor, happened to be an elected official.

Dr. Miller was a school board member, later a city council member, and finally the local chair of the Committee to Elect Senator Robert F. Kennedy. He introduced me to political leaders in the city and politicians that came from other cities. It was great to meet all the people who came to Dr. Miller's office. Often, I had to call other physicians, political leaders, and corporate leaders with whom Dr. Miller needed to conduct business. While many of these folks were white, most of them were Black. I had never been around so many Black professionals before. It was one of the best things that could have happened to me because it helped me realize I needed to find out what I was doing on this earth and how I could be as free as they seemed to be.

Dr. Miller helped me awaken to a political consciousness. Since I was eager to learn, he talked about political and social issues that concerned him. Watching him engage the political arena as a surgeon rather than as a full-blown politician gave me a sense of possibility. It made me think about trying to do something in the world other than simply surviving. He helped me to see myself as an African American with responsibility to understand the world I lived in and to be aware that I could openly resist the things I thought were wrong. I could speak and act. Though it would take me years to live more fully into what I learned, the seeds that were planted during this time eventually sprouted. Instead of just focusing on my own survival, I realized I could connect with other people like me, working African Americans who were also struggling to survive. I was on the path of discerning what I should do with my life. Meeting Dr. Miller, and having his support, was an important first step.

Dr. Miller was the first doctor to attend to Senator Robert F. Kennedy when Kennedy was shot in Los Angeles after the presidential primary in California. Kennedy had just won that primary, and those of us who supported him had so much hope. I wasn't there, but it was a devastating experience for Dr. Miller. He told me he was so sorry that the senator was gone. He had high hopes for his presidency just like all the rest of us. After Kennedy's assassination, I was not interested in many elections for a good while. It was devastating to lose him—and the energy and possibilities that he embodied.

Nineteen sixty-eight was, of course, a devastating year. We lost Dr. Martin Luther King Jr. in April and Robert Kennedy in June. I still remember the day when Dr. King was shot. I was sitting at my workstation in Dr. Miller's office. The announcement came on as a program interruption to the music station we typically played. Dr. Miller came from his office to the door of my area and said, "I think I want to go to Memphis. I might be able to help him." We paused in horror, thinking about what we could do. But within a few more minutes we heard the horrible fact that Dr. King was dead. We were immobilized. We managed to finish up the workday, going on with our respective tasks, but our hearts were weighted to the ground.

During that time, I kept myself extremely busy with work and school and a few church activities on Sunday. I was now able to attend a Church of Christ because my brother and his family were members of one.

Pepperdine Los Angeles, where I completed my undergraduate work, was a Church of Christ–affiliated school. I was glad to be on a Christian college campus because I had imagined it would be a more supportive place and that I would be able to find more people who were like me in terms of seeking a deeper faith. I was mistaken. The campus culture was not that different from the one at Compton College; we just had mandatory chapel on Wednesday, which was often not very inspiring. I started at Pepperdine in the fall of 1967 and graduated in December 1970. It is amazing how much happened in that short time span.

At Pepperdine, I met five people who had a huge impact on my life: Dr. Jennings Davis and his wife, Vera; Dr. Lucile Todd and her husband, Bill; and Ann King. These were five white people who helped me see that God had indeed made white people and did not sanction the hierarchies they imposed on society. Before this point, I hadn't ever allowed myself to ponder the question of how white people had come to see the world as they did. I knew that white people seemed to conclude that the world belonged only to them. However, I took their conclusion as a simple fact, no different from anything I'd observe in the natural world. It had never occurred to me to question racial separation and hierarchies. I had not gotten to the point of self-interrogation that allowed for such a query.

Instead, my lived experience had taught me to respect the racial separation we had in Arkansas and across the South—

and in many other parts of the United States, including California. I had decided that white people had nothing to do with me and I nothing to do with them. However, circumstances caused these five people at Pepperdine to engage with me. This made me have to rethink the ideas I had about white folks and what we had to do with one another.

I had the good fortune to work in the Deans of Students Office with Drs. Todd and Davis. I gravitated more toward Dr. Todd because she had an air about her that I had never experienced before. She was very calm, and though she spoke softly, there was a strength in her voice that was comforting to me. I didn't know her before coming to Pepperdine, but she seemed to know something about me. I was always glad to go to her office and do whatever tasks they had for me as the student worker. As time passed, she asked me to do more and more. She would find events that she thought were good for me to attend and get me a ticket. Sometimes it was a play, and sometimes it was a workshop or lecture. This developed over the two years that I worked in the office.

Dr. Todd had an African American woman friend named Ruby Holland who was a wonderful, Spirit-filled woman and deeply committed to healing the racial divide. She was a laywoman who worked tirelessly in the church and who simply glowed with kindness and care for others. And physically too, she was very beautiful. Ruby and Lucile organized programs about race together. Through their efforts, there was a group of Black and white women that gathered regularly. Lucile invited me to join. I think I was the only student. She must have seen something in me that made her believe this group would be good for me and I for them. She was correct. This group, called the Los Angeles Camp-In Group, was composed of women from the Church of Christ. Lucile and Ruby founded it to work for racial healing, and they made it a women's group because they believed women would get some of that work done if they could only get to know one another.

The women met once a month to talk about their lives. They also discussed race and other social concerns. There were usually twenty to thirty women present. They were all welcoming to me. They usually had a grand lunch. Then they spent the remainder of the time sharing, praying, and engaging in whatever other planned activity they had for the day. They spent weekends together as well. I was shocked. I had never seen Black and white people together in this way. I had never heard them talking to one another in the ways these women talked to one another. It was so unsettling for me. But my soul was thirsty for the kind of connection they seemed to enjoy. I wondered how that could happen.

One Saturday when the group was meeting, one of the oldest members told a story about a memory she had. She had been a child on a plantation where the children were fed in a trough, like the ones that the pigs' food was put in each day. She spoke about this dehumanizing experience as if it had happened just the other day. We heard the story and were overwhelmed with emotion. The meeting ended and we went home. But a few months later, at another meeting of the group, a young white woman said she wanted to wash the feet of the older woman who had shared the pig trough story earlier in the year. It took a while to get the older woman to agree to let her do it, but she finally agreed.

The young white woman knelt in front of the older Black woman and began washing her feet. The white woman began to cry, and as she did, the older woman said, "Don't cry. I want you to know that I don't hold anything against you because of all those things that happened to me when I was a child and the way that we were treated as children." By then all of us were crying. We were so inspired. This was one of the most powerful moments I ever experienced. I caught a glimpse of how healing could happen. I didn't know it was possible. I wondered if it could happen for me. On some deep intuitive level, I understood that I was carrying a lot of wounds and didn't know what to do with them. I wondered if a day could come when some of the burden might be lifted.

During my time at Pepperdine, another event shaped my understanding of race and of myself. This was the murder, on our campus, of fifteen-year-old Larry D. Kimmons on March 12, 1969. Larry was one of the boys from the neighborhood, all of them Black, who came to play basketball in the Pepperdine gymnasium. Larry's mother had come to Pepperdine to see if it was all right for him to be on the campus and for him and his friends to play basketball. Campus security had assured her that it was fine.

But one particular night, the white security guard—who was too old to be charged with that job, especially given the changing neighborhood—decided they were not allowed to play basketball. Those who witnessed the incident report that the guard told the boys to leave. Larry was trying to explain who they were and asked whether the security guard remembered his mother coming to the campus to talk to the officials in the gym. The security guard answered with a shotgun blast to this young man's body. Larry died on the scene.

I was home when the call came from my friend. I needed to begin praying, she said. She told me about the terrible tragedy—Larry Kimmons's murder—that had happened on campus. I had no idea what it might be like when I got there. I was in shock. I got into my car and drove to campus.

I found my friend. There were other students, reporters, neighbors, and administrators around. So much conversation and nothing that made any difference because this innocent child was dead and no one could do one thing about it. We felt as if a part of us died that night. After all, we were only a few years older than Larry. We knew his death was calling us forward to be whatever we needed to be. Our age could not be a factor. We simply had to step up to the task, and we did.

The fact of the matter is that Pepperdine should not have had an elderly white man with a shotgun as their security guard. This was during a time of major changes across the country and after the Watts Revolt, so white people were incredibly insecure about any group of Black folks that they had to engage. Mrs. Kimmons thought she had done enough by coming to campus to speak to someone. However, she had no way of knowing that responsible behavior could not address the racism that was walking around with the security guard. There is not a lot to say about this man. He was an elderly white man in a neighborhood that was becoming Blacker every day. He had no business being in that job, and if he was going to be on the campus, he had no business with a shotgun. What college campus allows a security guard to carry a shotgun anyway? This was wrong on so many levels.

Instead of the college president, vice president, and chancellor standing up for what was right, they were busy scrambling to find a way to make Larry Kimmons into a monster that deserved to die. But we students were declaring, "Hell no, not on our watch." We were going to hold the administration's feet to the fire until they did right by the Kimmons family, and it was going to begin with them going to Mrs. Kimmons's home and telling them that they gave somebody a license to kill and that he had killed her son. The president and vice president did not want to go, but it was fairly clear to them that they were between an immovable rock and a boulder. We were angry and not ready to have the usual games played that night.

The events that took place over the next few weeks are a blur in my memory, but there are threads that were woven into my soul never to be forgotten. One was Pepperdine's effort to make Larry into a monster in order to relieve itself of as much responsibility as possible. But our Black student vigilance would not abide this slander. We protested and made written demands that the university step up to the plate. We demanded they send a representative to go visit Mrs. Kimmons, pay for Larry's funeral, and provide some type of compensation for his siblings to attend Pepperdine. We didn't know anything, really, because Mrs. Kimmons should have sued them for the wrongful death of her son. Before this point, the university had refused to offer Mrs. Kimmons condolences. I'm sure they were far more concerned about liability than about doing what was right.

On the day of Larry's funeral, we sat packed shoulder to shoulder at a small church. I heard Larry's mother scream as she viewed her sweet child's lifeless body. I will never forget that scream. I don't want to forget it. Mrs. Kimmons's scream opened a space in my soul. This space in my soul will never find comfort until this country becomes a place where beautiful boys like Larry are not killed by white men who are frightened about having to learn to live in the world with folks they don't deem worthy of freedom and equality. I went to visit Mrs. Kimmons as much as I could until I left Los Angeles. Most of the time when I visited, she would be in bed. She never recovered. I was glad to go and visit and just be there with her, but I left feeling sad. But those visits helped me clarify a way I wanted to be in the world. I was not going to rest until I was sure I had done all I could to make this country safe for Black people and especially young Black boys. Even after I left Los Angeles, Mrs. Kimmons was never far from my thoughts.

Another thread woven into my soul is the reaction of the folks in my Church of Christ congregation, which had only Black members. I went to Bible class following Larry's murder and told the other attendees that we were struggling to make sure Pepperdine did right by the Kimmons family. I told them I was worried. They told me to stay home until the trouble was over. The pastor's wife told me that "my education was making me crazy." Perhaps she was afraid for me and thought I might get hurt, but I think it was mostly that she didn't want to see the boat being rocked because she was comfortable with her good, solid, middle-class life. However, there was one brother there whom I will always remember. He offered to come to campus with me if I thought that would help. He sounded like a Christian to me. I told him I would let him know. He didn't have to come, but his offer made a major difference to me.

During this time, I was a regular participant in a house church group that was composed mostly of young white people looking for an alternative to more conservative organized religion, who had decided that their understanding of a radical Jesus was the answer to everything. They were some of racism's best ambassadors because they wanted to be in the "I don't see race" world and never deal with the racism in the United States or in themselves. The unconscious racist is by far more dangerous than the overt racist. One cannot cover up racism with Jesus. My voice around all of this was very weak during this time, but I was quite clear that the Jesus that I knew demanded me to be in the conversations, struggles, protest, and disruption caused by Larry's murder. There was not going to be any "let's put this all behind us and turn to Jesus." The issues around this murder had to be addressed, and anyone who claimed to be a follower of Jesus needed to step up as near as I could tell.

The house church group members were not so happy with me and my disregard of their notions about what we should do. I knew what I had to do, and I was going to do it. This awakening was good for me. I needed to move away from this group. I figured out that they were patriarchal and racist and did not know it. They also had no interest in interrogating themselves. They were quite busy taking their respective places in the white supremacist, patriarchal, religious world and covering it all up with Jesus. Theirs was a Jesus that had nothing to do with me. I had come to the realization that Jesus was interested in my liberation as a Black woman walking around, as well as in my soul. It was about time for me to take an interest in both as well. Standing in solidarity around Larry's murder was my first big step in that direction.

After graduation, I continued to work for Dr. Miller and read a lot. One of the big things I did during that time was travel by bus to Berkeley, California, to meet the newly elected mayor, Warren Widener, who was the first African American to hold that post in that city. It was important to me. He was so gracious to spend time meeting with me, though I didn't have a lot to say to him. He told me that the all-Black janitorial staff at the office had voiced how much his presence meant to them. They told him that they stood a little taller when he walked in each day. The trip to Berkeley was a pilgrimage for me. I had never done anything like that before and haven't since. Finding the courage to make this trek was expressive of an internal shift that surprised me. I was beginning to see myself as someone who could reach out to powerful people—and who had something to talk about with them. I was also beginning to listen more to the voice of discernment, even when I didn't fully understand that voice myself. Some of my family knew I was going to Berkeley, but it didn't make much sense to them, and quite frankly, it didn't make much sense to me either. But I knew I had to do it. Upon my return, the voice of discernment was a little louder. I realized this change in me had begun even before I met Dr. Miller. I had first identified this voice as a young person in Arkansas, as I stepped out the backdoor and watched the sun rise alone. Although I couldn't describe my experiences in words, I was opening up that space in myself. Now I was quite clear that I had something to do in this world. My biggest challenge would be finding out what it might be.

5

The Wilderness

WHEN I LEFT ARKANSAS FOR LOS ANGELES, I vowed never to come back to the South to live. But in 1970, when I was twenty-four years old, I went against my vow and decided to move to Atlanta, Georgia. My family, especially my mother, was horrified. Who moves back to the South after escaping segregation, second-rate schools, poverty, white people making you invisible, and all the other aspects of racial apartheid? I was asked that question by people I met when I arrived in Georgia. When you are fortunate enough to vacate the South, what on earth would make you want to come back? In some ways the answer to these questions was very unformed for me, but in other ways it was clear. I had to return. The same energy that got me to get on a bus and travel to Berkeley helped me to pack all my belongings in an old Valiant that should not have been driven across town, let alone cross-country, and head for Atlanta.

Through my Church of Christ connections, I met a preacher from Atlanta who listened to me talk about moving to the South and invited me to come and stay with his family. He told me they had a lovely basement area that would work well for me. I was thrilled to have a temporary place to stay until I could find a job and get settled. Though I had worked for six years as a receptionist/office manager, I didn't have many other skills that would help me to find work. But I had confidence that I would find work when I got to Atlanta.

My mother insisted on traveling with me as far as Arkansas. She had been recruited to teach in Bakersfield, California, and relocated there. This move was a result of her unlawful firing in Arkansas, and a subsequent lawsuit. Her little elementary school in Arkansas had six or seven Black teachers and all of them were fired and replaced by white teachers. This was considered an act of discrimination, and the Black teachers surprised everyone by bringing a lawsuit against the district. It was an even bigger surprise that they won. They were offered their jobs back, but no one took the offer. They received back pay and some money to pay for relocating to other jobs.

My mother's eldest sister also was visting in California at the time that I was moving to Georgia, and she also was ready to ride with me. A part of her and my mother's motivation to accompany me was that they didn't think I should drive from California to Georgia alone. They were probably right about that. At the time, it was not safe for a woman—particularly a Black woman—to make this sort of trip by herself, but I was young and full of hope, courage, and inspiration for the adventure that I believed to be ahead of me. The car we traveled in was truly a wreck. Two mechanic friends of mine had gotten me the car and had assured me it was fine for the trip. I believed them. It takes my breath away, remembering how two grown men, one white and one Black, both of whom claimed to be my friends, encouraged me to embark on such a long and arduous journey across the country in a car that was so unfit for travel. Of course, I have to admit that I was courageous enough to do it. I didn't have any other way to get from California to Georgia, and I knew that I had to come to Georgia.

The first stop on the journey was my uncle's house in Yuma, Arizona. The old car's trunk didn't lock, so while I was at my uncle's house, I was robbed of the things that were in there. The robbers took my jewelry and my college diploma. I can't imagine what they would do with either the jewelry or my degree. The jewelry came mostly from secondhand stores and was pretty but not very valuable. I guess someone could change the name on the diploma and use it in some manner. I was sorry to lose my few possessions, but we had to carry on. I was surprised at the way I simply let it go.

We left before daylight to avoid the heat. I was the only driver, and I wanted to start early and rest in the early evening. The car had been fine from Los Angeles to Yuma. But after we left Yuma, the car used eight quarts of oil over twelve to fourteen hours of driving. I was horrified. I thought we would get stranded on the road while we were crossing the desert in our little car that was better suited for the junkyard than the road. I imagined us baking in the sun, our car a useless pile of metal by the side of the road. I feared I'd never see Georgia after all.

When we stopped for the evening, I called one of the mechanics who had told me we would be all right traveling in the car. He seemed somewhat puzzled but not particularly concerned about what might happen to us. He told me to keep putting in oil. I did this for the remainder of the trip, and we held our breath until we arrived in Arkansas. I left my mother and aunt there and was joined by my niece and nephew in Grambling, Louisiana, for the drive from there to Georgia.

Though I had lived for eight years in Los Angeles, it was challenging finding my way around in Atlanta. I had no idea what to expect in terms of the layout of the city. The roads were confusing and the traffic was worse than I had expected. This, of course, was in the days before GPS, so I did a fair amount of unnecessary driving, unintentional sight-seeing, and sometimes frantic searching for the path to my destination. I unfolded maps and scrutinized the names of streets. I also had to rely on directions given to me by the pastor I'd be staying with, and other friends. I drove around, double-checking the directions, unsure whether to turn left or right.

Eventually I arrived at the pastor's house and settled into the basement. Their house was lovely, and the basement was huge. I had a bedroom, sitting area, and bathroom along with a couple of other rooms. After living for a couple of years in a one-bedroom apartment with a roommate, this place felt like a mansion. But I was not prepared for how lonely I would be after my niece and nephew departed to return to Louisiana.

The pastor and his family were amazingly hospitable. His children were good to be accepting of a stranger coming to share their space. I was a little uncomfortable because I had never lived with anyone without paying them money. They were extraordinarily generous, and I stayed with them for close to five months. I would not have been able to get started in Georgia without their generosity. I worked on jobs that a temp agency sent me to do. This involved more driving around the unfamiliar streets of Atlanta. The pay for the temp jobs was not good, but I managed to buy gas and take care of basics. I hunted for a steady job as diligently as I could, as I wanted to be able to get my own place and to be independent as I was used to taking care of myself.

I had friends in Macon, Georgia, who worked in the public mental health world. I visited them once or twice while I still lived with the Atlanta family. On one of those visits, my friend informed me that the state of Georgia was hiring folks with liberal arts backgrounds to work in the mental health system. They were trying out this new approach, hoping to attract more people, and people with a range of experiences, to jobs in the mental health field. My friend suggested that I apply for a technician position, working directly with patients in the mental health system. I wasn't sure if I could do that work, but I was certainly willing to find out. I got all the necessary information regarding the job and submitted an application immediately. I was overjoyed to learn that I qualified as a social work technician and that the state of Georgia was pleased to offer me that position.

I had to move to Macon for the new job. I wanted to live in one of the opulent old houses that had been renovated and turned into apartments, as they were far more spacious and had more character than the newer apartments. They had fireplaces and large bathtubs that were great for long aromatic soaks with oils and herbs. Since I tend to like vintage items better than newer, more modern things, the old apartments were appealing. But I was not able to find one that would rent to a Black person. Every day, I checked the newspaper for lists of vacant apartments. Then I trekked from place to place, simply to be told that the place had been rented. I finally remembered that I was back in the place I vowed to stay away from for the remainder of my life. I wondered what I was doing here. I had hoped to be welcomed by Julian Bond's New South. I wasn't sure where the New South was, but it certainly wasn't in Macon. After reading *Black Rebel*, a biography of Julian Bond, I expected the South to be more accommodating. My first mistake was thinking that Macon and Atlanta would be similar. Atlanta was at least fifty years more progressive than Macon. Black people had enjoyed a completely different set of experiences in terms of being more empowered in Atlanta, even though it was not like Los Angeles. But in Macon, there were times when it seemed that I was not even in the same state that housed Atlanta. There was a completely different kind of energy there. But I was still relieved to have a job and a little more independence than I had when living with the kind souls in Atlanta who had been so generous to me.

I ended up moving into North Napier Apartments. The complex was relatively new, and most of the units in my building were still empty. The place came with kitchen appliances but no furniture. I bought a bed and a dresser, and one chair for the living room. I would have to wait for my first paycheck from my new job before getting any more furniture. It was fine with me. While I had no clue what was ahead of me, I thought it would be better than what was behind me.

There were four of us hired as technicians for the mental health center in Macon. Three of us were social work techs and one was a psychology tech because his undergraduate major was psychology; both positions required us to counsel patients seeking mental health care. While the building we worked in was old, it was good enough, and each of us had a nice office. I was the only African American on the mental health staff, and there was one African American nurse on the physical health side. Ninety percent of the patients were African American, and the majority of them were struggling with extreme poverty. Many were recent residents of the old state hospital, Central State Mental Institution, who had been discharged when the state decided to clear out that facility of the mentally ill and replace them with prisoners. Many of the folks there were not ready for discharge but were discharged anyway. At the Central State Mental Institution, patients were subjected to electric shock treatment and lobotomies. The institution had also been the subject of an exposé that reported patients being given psychotropic drugs without consent, a nurse performing major surgery without oversight, and staff being drunk while supervising patients.

Macon's entire mental health system was fraught, with much to lament. One needs more than intuition and a good heart to be an effective therapist. In particular, although I didn't exactly realize it at the time, training and mentorship are the two most important things for new therapists to have. Of course, this was exactly what the state of Georgia didn't provide for us. Without proper training, until I learned some things while on the job, I didn't know much about how to help people. I was able to listen, and I was compassionate; those two things helped me. But my lack of training and experience often impacted my performance. And caused me to be traumatized by the plight of the patients I was charged to counsel.

Racism was a serious issue in the clinic because several of the psychiatrists came from Cuba as refugees from the Castro regime. They didn't really know anything about African Americans, and they were not very respectful of their patients. Most of their practice with these folks was confined to drug therapy. Their patients were not very functional. They were often seen in large groups, as the psychiatrists did not try any type of individualized talk therapy or mental health interventions. Along with this dynamic, there was a different group of folks that the psychiatrists had decided to work with more, in terms of actually doing talking sessions and supporting treatment with drugs. I was never totally clear on how they made their selections, but I think it had to do with their assessing patients as more likely to benefit from both instead of only having drugs. It was not a good system. Our job as the new techs was to lighten the load of the regular staff psychiatrists by taking on some of their cases. The biggest problem we had was that we had no idea what we were doing. We had no background in mental health and no formal training. Despite this, we learned on the job as we worked with senior staff and gradually began to have our own list of patients to see.

As a child, I had lived in a world of silences, dominated by unspoken fears. Now, as a mental health technician, I was expected to invite people out of silence, into sharing. The job was an opportunity to encourage others to tell the truth about their lives. The work became all-consuming to me. The African American patients knew I was not from Georgia. When they asked where I was from and heard "Los Angeles," they wanted to know what brought me to Macon. They wondered what was wrong with me, relocating from California to Georgia on purpose. The white patients didn't seem to mind working with me. However, most of the time when I worked with someone who was white, I had a senior-level licensed therapist working with me. When I was assigned African Americans, I was expected to work with them alone. I noticed this when I first began working there but didn't think much of it. Later, with greater discernment and an eye for the truth, I saw the entire pattern. Everyone on staff at the mental health clinic was racist. This included the white friends who had gotten me the job. Although they were from Los Angeles, they had fallen right into the racist rhythms of the Southern culture. They kept their heads down and did not rock any boats. They allowed all the African Americans, including me, to be invisible.

One incident from that time continues to be very vivid for me. There were several women staff members in the mental health division. One day, we were in the lounge when it was time for lunch, and one white staff member asked if folks wanted to go to lunch together. Everyone agreed that was a good idea. There was discussion back and forth about where to go. Finally, one senior staff psychologist suggested the Club. Everyone thought that sounded fine. They all gathered up their things and departed. One of them turned and asked me if I was coming. The senior staff psychologist quickly yet casually said, "Oh, she can't come to the Club. They don't allow Blacks in there."

They went on their way, laughing, without a thought for what had just happened to me, or what would happen to me. I was left sitting in the lounge to eat lunch alone, or go someplace alone, or whatever—it didn't matter to them. I went home, which was not very far from my workplace. I was deeply hurt. Two of the women in the group had previously behaved as if we were friends. One of them had hosted me at her home. She had even told me my skin looked beautiful and asked me what skin care products I used. When I told her, she bought some of the same products, saying she was inspired by me. At the time, it was very unusual for a white woman to use skin care products recommended by a Black woman. In fact, it was very unusual for a white woman to take advice about beauty or anything else from a Black woman.

I thought one of these women, or perhaps both, would reach out after the group returned from lunch. I thought they'd come to see what I did for lunch or let me know that they regretted my being left out. It didn't happen; neither of them ever mentioned it. We simply acted as if I hadn't been slighted. Throughout my life, I had become used to tucking injuries away. I thought hiding the pain would make it easier for me to survive. When the women I had considered friends allowed me to be left behind, I did this yet again. I told myself it wasn't important, that I shouldn't let it distract me. Instead, I thought, I should keep my focus and simply get my work done. As I remember this incident now to write about it, I realize that none of them ever mentioned it because I was invisible in the first place, so they didn't really leave anyone in the room. After all, I was Black and should have been prepared for their behavior. I imagine they figured I would get over it because I had to be used to being left out.

CHAPTER 5

The Macon mental health clinic was one of the most toxic environments I could have found to work in. There were constant reminders that I didn't exist in the minds of my white coworkers. I don't remember anyone ever saying that I had done a good job. I was never complimented about anything. Over and over, skinny white women who showed up for work well dressed were touted as if they invented a new form of oxygen. Meanwhile, I sat there dressed just as well, and no one even acknowledged I was there, breathing the same air.

One day, one of the technicians who was part of the same cohort as I was took it upon herself to explain to me how she saw me. She must have been feeling particularly bold that day. Her assessment included a very caustic remark about my interest in achievement. She spoke about my being achievement-oriented as if it were a rare disease. She sounded angry. I'm not sure what prompted her to think she had any business talking to me about such things at all, but she felt entitled. Yes, I was interested in achieving. I had this interest because I was a human being, and like most human beings, I was on a long search for what I was to be doing on this planet. I suppose she didn't think I, a Black woman, would be interested in such pursuits. I was glad to be successful at tasks I took on and, frankly, did not see any reason to be different. She, on the other hand, regarded this basic human desire—to learn new things and to be successful—as something that only white people were allowed to have. Later as I watched her grabbing her bit of advancement, I wondered if she had any idea how she sounded talking to me that day. I didn't know about projection at that time, but now I understand that something in me made her uncomfortable, jealous or something, and she was speaking out of that space. No wonder I didn't understand; how could I? She was mostly talking about her own shadow side.

She said this on a day when that was the conversation I was least expecting to have with anyone. I really could not recover fast enough to say anything clever, and at the time, I wasn't used to speaking up to defend myself. So it was easier to let it go, and that is what I did. As I think back on it now, this woman was a major trespasser in my life. To further her own ambitions, she took what she could from me. First, like my former friend, she chose some of the same skin care products I used. She seemed to be striving to be the best she could be, and I watched her taking whatever cues she could from me in some of the staffing sessions of our patients' cases. And yet, at the same time, she denigrated me.

Trespassing white women are very problematic to African American women. They show up in our soul gardens and steal what they can of our energy, strength, relationships, behavior, and anything else they like, to enhance themselves. As Black women, we are a bit overly focused on white women connecting to Black men, but in actuality, other ways of trespassing might be more traumatizing. I think of instances in which white women have hijacked or pirated Black women's behaviors or ideas. Then they invite us into a conversation about the very thing they stole, or find ways to exhibit what they have stolen without ever admitting their theft or their desire to be like us. I didn't realize this was happening to me while I worked at the Macon mental health clinic. It had happened before, but it wasn't as impactful because the setting was not so desolate. No matter the setting, this is a traumatizing experience for Black women. It has happened to me since, and I have been much better able to process it and to make sure I called it by its ugly name.

The racism I experienced while working at the clinic was both subtle and obvious. One night, when all of us paraprofessionals were traveling together back home from a retreat, I was closing my eyes after the long, stressful day. The psychology tech, a native of Macon, believed I was asleep, so he felt comfortable calling African Americans "niggers" because that was the way he referred to Black people when he was alone with white folks. I pictured him talking to mentally ill African Americans, as he did every single day. Was he thinking this awful word while he was hearing their sad life stories? While he watched them break down into tears? While he wrote up their evaluations? I was mortified. And what did he think of me? I knew I should speak up and name the ugly truth of his racism. But I wasn't sure whom to tell, and I wasn't sure if anyone would listen.

It was difficult for me to admit how much I was struggling. So when I met the man I'll call Philip, I began to rely on him too much, rather than trusting my own discernment with the patients. Philip was a licensed therapist, so we worked closely with each other as he often was my supervisor. In general, my white coworkers had made me feel small and invisible. Philip saw me and listened to my concerns. Because of this, I saw him as someone who would rescue me from the silence that had dominated my life. I didn't realize, yet, that the ability to speak my truth—not the man I was speaking it to—was my real source of strength. Philip began to mentor me mostly by listening. He helped me with some of my cases that were particularly difficult and was mostly just a good friend. He showed kindness and concern for the stress I was experiencing. Beyond that, he was willing to engage me in some of the existential questions I had lived with all my life and had never asked anyone, such as: *Who am I? What am I doing here? Why does anything matter? What is death? Who is God? What does God really do? Why are Black people hated so much?* Until now, I had banished to silence these and so many other questions. Now I had a conversation partner, and I was thrilled, but it became too much for my coworker. He became overwhelmed.

One day, I knocked on Philip's door, as I had done for weeks, and began to talk about something. He started to tell me he couldn't keep being friends with me and that I was not to come to his office anymore. I was stunned. I had been enjoying the wonderful supportive energy he brought to our friendship for several months. I think, though I didn't know it at the time, that I was caught in a severe transference, which often happens in therapeutic settings. My sense of connection and dependence scared Philip and he didn't know what to do with it. I didn't know what to do with it either, but telling someone—seemingly out of nowhere—to go away, when that person has to work with you every day, is actually cruel. I was hurt, angry, disappointed, and dismayed. I felt lost.

Years later, I realized that this friend and coworker was actually in worse psychological shape than I was at the time. I was learning to speak the truth and ask hard questions, but some of those conversations were frightening to Philip, even though he never said so. Because I needed him to be a savior, I was unable to see the person right in front of me. Instead, I saw only my own needs. Philip had no capacity to save anyone—not even himself. But I was far too desperate for revelations, for someone to tell me something true about the world and my own experiences. At the time, I had no idea that the revelations I needed about myself could come only from me. I saw Philip as a far greater resource than he had the capacity to be, which pushed me to the verge of my own mental health breakdown. The fallout of this friendship made me severely depressed. However, I did as I'd always done, and stayed silent about my suffering. I managed to continue to function, going to and from work, navigating the toxic environment.

One day, a new psychiatrist arrived to work in the psychiatric unit of the hospital. It was clear that he would be engaged with the staff in the mental health clinic as well.

I liked him, and he seemed to regard me as a person, which was uncommon for the white people working there. He also sought my input on cases. This was because I understood mentally distraught young African Americans, and I especially understood the African American girls and young women. I worked well with them because they were trying to find out how to be free just as I was, and were seeking a place of acceptance as worthy human beings. We had a lot in common. I knew what it was to feel lost in the world and was able to reach out to these young women and girls who felt even more lost. A few of them became fairly stable and managed to move on with their lives. Although I didn't realize it at the time, I was practicing a skill that would be crucial as my journey continued: encouraging people to tell the difficult truth. The job was challenging, but I was good at working with the African American girls because I had something my white coworkers did not have. I had the belief that these girls had important stories to tell, and as a result, I had the ability to listen.

After I left that job, I came back to visit this psychiatrist. He told me he had wished for me to be present with several patients because he felt I could help them and he could not. I was glad to hear that because my time at that workplace was a source of deep trauma for me. But even within that trauma, there was a hopeful message. The psychiatrist I respected also respected me. In particular, he respected me for my ability to help people speak the hard truths of their lives. Although working at the clinic was a long and painful night in my life, the light of discernment did finally shine, revealing a flickering picture of who I was, and what I could be.

Those loving and kind relationships I had formed in college seemed a million miles away. The sense of confidence and agency I had developed during those last years at Pepperdine were getting smashed by daily doses of denigration and the lack of community. I had no base of support during this time.

Just at my lowest point, when I was certain I could take it no more, a friend in Macon invited me to move in with them. They were going to be moving away at the end of the school year, so I had a year to live with them. It was great having someone to be more connected to. I was ready for a change, so I took them up on their offer.

I finally realized that I had to get out of working in the mental health tech position or I would die. So I began to job-hunt. I had met a woman at Fort Valley State College who promised me a job with her as a research assistant. Fort Valley is about a thirty-minute drive from Macon, so it was relatively easy to go back and forth, but I wanted to find someplace closer to live. I found a house that was for rent. It was a mess, so I would go there often after clocking in a full day at the mental health center and work on the house with the notion that I would be moving there soon. I gave notice at the center with a great sense of joy and relief. I was so glad to be getting out of there. But a few days after I left my job, the professor at Fort Valley informed me that her grant funding did not come through. I was beyond devastated.

I decided I needed to leave Georgia and made the decision to move to Memphis. I had grown up sixty-five miles from Memphis in Moro, Arkansas, so going to Memphis felt in some ways as if I were going home. But I was in the same place I had been in when first moving back to the South: I needed to find a job. I drove to and from Memphis to job-search, without much success. I checked in with an impoverished school district in Mississippi about a teaching position, and that didn't work out. I came back to Georgia for a bit. I had paid to live in that horrible house in Fort Valley, Georgia, for one month, so I stayed there because the friends with whom I had been living in Macon were now moving.

I applied for a job with the Memphis City Schools as a social worker and was hired. I was delighted. My only furniture was my bedroom set and chair. I went to Memphis and managed to find a place to live with a woman who was a counselor in one of the schools. The work with the school system was much easier than what I had left at the mental health center. The environment, though toxic, was less so than at that previous job.

I had a few friends in Memphis, including a good friend from college, a white woman, who had demonstrated that a white person could love and respect me. I was glad to be near her. I started attending the Church of Christ that had sent folks to Brinkley to baptize me and my siblings when we were in high school. It was a bit weird to show up there and find that they still had the same pastor. He remembered the event but forgot my name. This confirmed the misgivings I had about them as a teenager: that they did not have any genuine interest in me. After a few times of attending this church, I realized it was not good enough. I was beginning to see my value and walk away from situations that would not be healthy for me. I left that congregation and went to a different Church of Christ. One of my coworkers attended this church, which was much better and made me feel more comfortable.

Things in Memphis were going well until one night I was awakened by all kinds of commotion outside the house. Someone was banging on the door and yelling for my room-mate. This scared me really badly. It brought me back to my childhood years in Moro, when we would have to wake up in the middle of the night and get dressed, fearing storms. I felt helpless, overwhelmed by that nameless fear. I got up to see if my roommate was awake, as I couldn't imagine that she could sleep through the noise. She was up, and she whispered to me that she didn't want the man outside to know she was here. I went back into my room and back to bed. That was simply the beginning. There were numerous other times when my roommate's unwanted boyfriend showed up in the middle of the night banging on the door, yelling for her to open it, calling her phone number and threatening to break the door down. I was scared whenever these incidents happened. After a bit, this roommate began to be antagonistic toward me. One night I came home and she confronted me about going to meet my friends for meals. She also accused me of wasting money. She had no legitimate reasons for bringing this up. It was my money and had nothing to do with her. I paid her what we had agreed on, and there was never any problem with the payments. I didn't realize at the time that she was simply envious of the life she imagined me to be living. It was only with time and perspective that I was able to recognize the fear behind her anger. She felt alone and resented me for having friends and an active social life. Eventually this escalated to her being upset if I left a glass on the sink or if I put too much food in the refrigerator. It was one thing and then another. One day I realized I could not keep putting my energy into this arrangement. She was not well, I realized, and I did not need to be there.

Yet again, I was scrambling to find a place to live. I wondered whether I would ever be able to feel settled somewhere. When my living situation became unbearable, I spoke to a coworker friend with whom I also attended church, asking if her parents would let me rent their spare room. Her parents were glad to do it. So I told my roommate I was moving out at the end of the week, though the month was not up yet. She was livid. I left the house not knowing if I would be able to get in to get my things when I got back. She got it together and didn't say anything further. She managed to be civil for those two days, knowing I would be moving. She accused me of breaking something I had not broken. Although I was frustrated by the situation, I left her money to replace it. I wanted to be completely free and clear of her. My instinct told me it would be best to avoid having people like this in my life. I was beginning to listen to my instinct and avoid people who would harm me. I did not tell her where I was going, though she asked me more than once. It was not information that she needed to have.

The year in Memphis proved to be good enough. In the summer of 1975 I went back to visit Macon. I decided to visit some folks I knew at Mercer University from the previous summer when, after quitting the mental health center, I had worked as a dormitory counselor for Upward Bound, a program designed to bring high school students to college campuses to help them get a sense of what college life is like. I went in to the see the dean of students because he was always very kind to me.

The dean asked me if I would like to come work with them in student life as the assistant dean of women. I guess I did a better job than I had imagined when I worked with Upward Bound. The catalyst for the dean's invitation didn't matter then and doesn't matter to me today. What matters is that there are times when things just come together and the unexpected shows up. I was floored. Yes, this was the job I dreamed of having. I wanted to be like my friend and mentor at Pepperdine, Dr. Lucile Todd. "Absolutely," I said. "When can I begin?" After our conversation, I walked through the campus looking at the students. They were so full of energy and hope for the future, reminding me of my own hopes for the future, my own openness to the possibilities of life. In the months of my struggles with finding work, and during my dark night of the soul—the period I spent working in that toxic, racist mental health center—I wondered whether I would ever find a place where I could do meaningful work, where I felt I belonged. It felt like I finally found the place I was meant to be.

While I have a wonderful capacity to imagine and to daydream, I try to stay grounded. Even before my meeting with the dean, I had come to realize that the job I wanted was one working with students. Of course, there is always an element of idealization in situations such as this because I had no way to really know what the daily hassles for this position would be. I had thought I would have to go to graduate school before getting a job like the one at Mercer. I wasn't excited about going back to school, so I hadn't pursued that kind of employment. However, I walked into the dean's invitation to come and take that job without having to do anything but say yes. I was beyond amazed. I'm not sure how the energy systems that have been set out in the universe work, but they make these things possible. I trust them regardless of whether they are called "God" or "angels" or what have you. The specifics do not concern me as much as my desire to stay in the flow of energy that leads to the positive rather than the negative.

The job at Mercer started in July 1975. The social work job with Memphis City Schools ended in late May. It was perfect. I told my supervisor I was returning to Macon and would be going to Mercer to become the assistant dean of women. He was not pleased to have to refill my position. He wanted to know why I didn't tell him sooner and then accused me of going from job to job since I had been there for only one school term. I simply looked at him and reiterated what I said. I was leaving, and he had no words nor enough money to change my mind. I knew Mercer was my next move. I had said yes to it, and nothing could deter me. I was a good social worker in the Memphis school system, and this director knew he would have a hard time finding another employee like me, but that was not my task to tackle.

That June, I loaded my bedroom furniture onto a trailer and headed east. This move to Macon was very different, and the circumstances were much better. First of all, I was to live in an apartment right on the Mercer campus. I was going to have a built-in community and not have to be out in the city experiencing an extreme sense of isolation. The apartment was small—one bedroom—but it was heavenly. It was painted and clean and ready to occupy. I got help getting my furniture in there. Then I made a trip to the secondhand store to find some additional furnishings. I bought a new deacon's bench and an old table. I also bought a kitchen table and four kitchen chairs that had many layers of paint on them. I could imagine the set with a new paint job being exactly what I wanted. Once home, I got to work on transforming the kitchen set. It was a sign to me of fresh starts and new opportunities. This was just what my weary soul needed.

It took me far more days and much harder work than I was anticipating to get the multiple layers of paint off the table and chairs, but I finally got it done. Then I painted them a bright yellow. They were gorgeous. I was very proud of myself. Later someone gave me a couch that was in good condition and large enough for someone to sleep on so that I could actually have an overnight guest if the person was not too particular about sleeping quarters. After I was at Mercer for a while, my apartment became a respite spot for students. So many students slept on that couch before I finally discarded it for a better one years later. There were several students whom I trusted to stay in my apartment for a little retreat when I was out of town.

For the most part, I felt welcome at Mercer. There was one woman working in the Student Life Office who was racist. I would learn later that she refused to go out to birthday lunches or to participate in any of the office social gatherings after I came on board because she didn't want to socialize with a Black person. She was always polite and never did anything that depicted distaste for me as a Black person, though she was not especially friendly or welcoming. She was somewhat aloof. She had worked out in her head a formula that helped her navigate her racism. She had to work with Black people, so she would behave in order to keep her job, but she was not going to socialize with us. Of course, there were other racists at Mercer. There were several "good old boy" types on the faculty who wanted to take me under their wings so I could become their designated token Negro. The designated Negro is someone who enjoys what looks like a favored place, but it is merely an illusion because in the final analysis it becomes denigrating and dehumanizing. The one holding such a place is no more than a pawn in the white supremacy paradigm. That was not going to be my plight.

I resisted them. I was not looking to fill that space for anyone because I was looking for freedom. They didn't understand that I was not a candidate for the position of designated Negro until they had a chance to live around me for a while. Then they learned I was a young woman on a mission to be liberated and to share liberation with anyone who was seeking it. I was on a quest and a lifelong pilgrimage to find out who I was and how to be free, and no one was going to stop me.

My job as assistant dean of women at Mercer was thrilling. I enjoyed gearing up for school, particularly getting the dormitories ready, because I was in charge of women's housing. I looked forward to the students returning and to the many programs we would be offering during the school year. I thrived in the fast-paced action. After my first semester, I began to teach in the first-year seminar that all first-year students were required to take. There were several different topics offered each year, having to do with issues such as the environment, justice, economics, climate, prisons, health, and more. It was an even greater delight to work with students and to attend all the programs associated with the seminars. We brought in amazing thinkers and speakers such as Ralph Nader, Nikki Giovanni, and Maya Angelou to help our first-year students to become more critical thinkers. It was stimulating and intimidating to be in the staffing sessions with my more seasoned colleagues, but I held my own. While I was not the teacher I would become, I managed to teach my students and to bring enough disrupting energy to challenge their presuppositions and their places of comfort. I used the task of teaching to get them moving in good directions toward formulating and asking better questions.

One of our first-year seminars was on the topic of scarcity on the planet in relation to food, water, fuel, clean air, and other essential natural resources. We read all the latest books on the topic. We brought in remarkable speakers and screened powerful films. We all learned about how Americans were making too many poor decisions regarding the environment and food sources. We also learned about the devastating impact of not developing good public transportation systems so that we could cut back on automobile ownership. We had Ralph Nader come as a speaker. He added to our unrest. Sometime soon after, I remember thinking, "I am going to go somewhere and get a nice big hamburger"—but then I thought about the implications of that choice and refrained. By the end of some of those conversations, all of us wanted to go hide until someone fixed the world and invited us back to the table. We felt helpless, facing these insurmountable problems. However, I knew that speaking about them together, and naming them together, would empower the younger generation to work toward changing some of these systems.

While my work with the first-year seminars and as assistant dean of women was going well for the first few years, I was not doing well. I didn't have as strong of a personal support community as I needed, even though I was surrounded by my colleagues, with whom I had a decent enough relationship, and the students. I felt the desolation of being in the midst of my personal quest while living in a predominantly white community that was not able to comprehend me or my needs in any manner. I was doing the best I could, but a deep sense of loneliness and heart hunger accompanied me on a daily basis because I could not separate myself from the sense of being invisible. While no one at Mercer was openly racist or abusive, it was clear that no one was spending much time or effort trying to truly see me. I was one of seven African American professionals on the campus, and none of us was making much of an effort to be seen as individuals. Most of our energy was focused on the campus climate and the particular ways in which race and race relations impacted that climate.

At Mercer, we formed a Black professional caucus to help us be recognized as a group since individual recognition was so lacking. That generated a fair amount of concern among our white colleagues, as was often the case in the late sixties and seventies when groups of Black people decided to organize for any reason. Thus, our public face was always turned toward civil and human rights issues, and more particularly to the issues on campus related to race, without much desire or opportunity for any one person to be very transparent about their personal life. I kept my personal journey to myself, and it resulted in my being desperately lonely during those early years as an administrator and instructor. In this atmosphere, I continued my search for a path to inner peace and rest.

One Sunday afternoon in the fall of 1979, the search led me to the local library to browse. I found a copy of an old *Life* magazine that listed ten of America's greatest preachers. The list included Howard Thurman. I had never heard of him but was very drawn to his biographical sketch. At that time, he had written about twenty books. He cofounded and had led an ecumenical, interracial faith community in San Francisco called the Fellowship Church for All Peoples. After reading about him, I went on a search to find some of the things he had written. I was pleased to find several of his books in the library. I checked them all out that day. When I returned to my apartment, I began to read and found myself simply devouring the meditations he had penned. I had not ever read anyone who sounded like him—especially not anyone of African descent. I was captivated by every word on the page.

I felt that Dr. Thurman's work had been sent to me to answer some of the questions about my own journey. On the day I discovered Dr. Thurman, God heard the cry of my soul. Dr. Thurman proclaimed so beautifully that God always hears the person who is praying, no matter whether what you are praying about comes into being or not. I knew I had to do more than merely read this amazing person, but I wasn't sure what I should do. My first response was to write to him, so I did. I wasn't sure he would receive my letter because it was not that simple to find out where to send it. But I managed to get an address for him in San Francisco, where he lived with his lovely wife, Sue Bailey Thurman. As it turned out, Dr. Thurman did receive my letter, and he took the time to respond. In his beautifully written response, he invited me to hear him at Spelman College in Atlanta in May 1980, where he would be delivering the baccalaureate address. I was delighted.

When the time came for the baccalaureate service at Spelman, I was excited and a bit nervous about the possibility of meeting the person who penned such amazing wisdom and with whom I felt a great sense of kinship. I wondered what on earth I would say to him. It wasn't easy for me to talk to people I didn't know. I am an introvert. Nevertheless, my soul knew that the appointment with Howard Thurman in May 1980 was one not to be missed.

I drove to Atlanta and found my way to Sisters Chapel on the Spelman campus, where I got a seat close to the front so that I could introduce myself following the service. When Dr. Thurman took the microphone and began to recite the 139th Psalm, I found that my anxiety about meeting him began to lessen. By the time he finished his sermon, I had forgotten all about my anxiety. I was so thankful to have heard him and to be in his presence. Through stories and insight, he conveyed a powerful message regarding the necessity to search for the genuine in your life. He gave me a sense of confidence and hope that I had not experienced before that moment.

When I went up to introduce myself to Dr. Thurman at the proper time, I spoke to him out of a great place of gratitude. His response to me was one of sheer graciousness. He had the most amazing manner of making it seem as if he had known me for many years, though he was meeting me for the first time. He invited me to come meet with him the following day. I was ecstatic. As I drove back to Macon, I had a deep sense that a major shift was about to occur for me. I could hardly wait for the next day to arrive. I knew I had met a person who would accompany me for the remainder of my life. I was correct. My first encounter with Dr. Thurman was more than four decades ago, and the continued journey with him has led me to many others who have found his wisdom to be a mainstay in their lives. His teachings have helped me as I have continued to search for the genuine for myself.

Toward the end of 1980, I went to California to visit my family and made the wise choice to go to San Francisco to visit Dr. Thurman. He graciously welcomed me into his home there as he had done at Spelman earlier that year. Dr. Thurman died in 1981, and I will never cease to be grateful for the gift of his presence in my life. I think about him every day and quote him on most days, especially if I'm teaching or preaching.

My experience with Dr. Thurman taught me to stay open to the process of listening to my heart and head as I walk on my pilgrim pathway. This was the behavior that he modeled so beautifully. I was no longer the little girl frightened of mist and storms, beset by illnesses I didn't understand. I was more able to look around and see the truth of things. The following story will demonstrate better what I mean.

When I returned to Macon, I wanted to have a better church community, so I drove to Atlanta each Sunday to a very high-spirited Church of Christ. While it was a good experience to be there on Sundays with everyone, there were times when I was simply too tired to make the drive. One Sunday I visited a church that was recommended to me by folks I had eaten dinner with on Saturday night. It was Northside Christian Church, a white church.

I arrived when they were singing the opening hymn. While I was waiting in the lobby for an opportune time to enter, a group of ten white men, all walking in a line like schoolchildren going out to recess, approached me. One of them, the leader in the front of the line, asked, "Who are you and what is your business here?" I thought that seemed like such a strange question. I began to respond by saying that some friends had invited me. But before I could finish the sentence, he said, "You don't have any friends here." Finally, it dawned on me that they didn't allow Black people there. I could see the truth, and I was not afraid to name it. So I asked him whether Black people were allowed to worship there, and he said, "No, we don't allow Black people." I turned and walked out and got into my car as fast as I could. I burst into tears there in the driver's seat. No one had ever thrown me out of a church house before. I had done nothing but show up, and I had been invited by people who went there and who really had no idea their church was practicing that kind of racism. I took off down the road.

As I was driving back home, three of the most beautiful deer I have ever seen popped out of the woods. One ran across the road. I stopped, and that one was followed by another one, and then a third. They were in a hurry to cross the road, which was a good thing because quick traffic and distracted drivers are dangerous for deer. Their appearance reminded me of the Father/Mother, Son, and Spirit. I just pulled my car over to the side of the road and sat for a bit.

The pastor from Northside called me that afternoon. He apologized and asked how I was. "I'm fine," I said. "But your church is not fine as long as there are folks there who think the church belongs to them, and who don't think any Black people are welcome." He asked if he could come visit me, probably because he knew he should, and probably because he felt guilty. I said he could. I was hoping he would be able to speak the truth about the situation and that, through this, he could heal the breach he had allowed to be possible in his congregation. Over the next month, I learned that he did come by, but only at a time I had indicated I wouldn't be home. After that happened a couple of times, I called him and told him to make and keep an appointment with me or forget about it. I was beginning to see that there was no genuine desire for healing in his heart. He finally came by at a time when I was home. The conversation was not very fruitful. I thought back to my childhood, when I was so afraid of storms because I didn't understand what was truly happening. After my conversation with the pastor, I could see the truth of the situation, and I could see what was actually in his heart. He seemed very shocked by what had happened and tried to make it sound as if he had no idea that such a thing could happen in this congregation. But here he was, a man serving as the pastor of a church filled with many folks who were racist enough to support a policy that stated that they did not allow Black people to worship with them and he did not know that they were like that, and he had the audacity to say that they never had a problem before the Sunday that I showed up there. And he wanted me to believe that he was not like them. But after the initial shock wore off, I was surprised to realize that I was not too bothered by the whole affair. I realized I had made great strides toward not being afraid to know and face the truth.

6

Metamorphosis

AROUND 1979, WHEN I HAD BEEN at Mercer as assistant dean of women for almost five years, I realized it was a disadvantage that I had not gone to graduate school. I was very good at my job. The degree most likely would not have helped me to do better work, and the university knew I had only an undergraduate degree and was not worried when they hired me. However, I knew that not having an advanced degree would become an issue in the long run, so I decided to do something about it. I had done social work more than anything else, and I was beginning to be good at it. I enjoyed listening to people, and I had a good ear to hear the layered stories that were brought to me. Because of this, I decided to pursue a master's in social work. I looked into it and found an accelerated program at Atlanta University. The previous work I had done in the field made me eligible, and I could complete the program in eleven months instead of twenty-four. I decided it was a good fit for me.

The program would require me, though, to be away from Macon in the summer of 1980 because I needed to be a full-time student during those months, and I could not commute the ninety minutes from Macon to Atlanta. The administration of Mercer was very cooperative and agreed for me to have the summer of 1980 off with full salary. In the fall, I attended evening classes for my graduate program and was able to teach a bit at Mercer during the days. As part of my master's program, I had to complete an internship, so during that period, I taught at Mercer one day a week, and it all worked out. It was a grueling schedule at times, but I was able to get through that MSW program with full salary. I was grateful to not have the stress of trying to find ways to pay bills while studying. I graduated from the program in May 1981.

Mama took the bus from California to be in Macon for my graduation ceremony. She was good about showing up as much as possible for all of us, although she was still teaching and had limited time for traveling. Though we didn't talk about it, she must have been amazed that a child of hers was getting a second college degree when it had taken her eighteen years to get one. She made it clear that she was proud of me by being willing to come all the way to Georgia for graduation.

Along with my work as assistant dean of women, I was directing the African American studies program, mostly by default, because there was no one to take it over when the professor who directed it took another job in 1977. It was an interdisciplinary program by necessity. Mercer never provided enough funding for it because it was not considered a viable part of the curriculum. That we had the program at all was just a superficial gesture to make Mercer look better and to keep the Black students and faculty quiet during a time when many university students were protesting for ethnic studies and Black studies courses.

The African American studies program at Mercer offered a major but had no faculty and a very small budget. Clearly, it was an initiative that no one was trying to see thrive. When I began leading the program, I thought it should be more viable. Because there was no full-time staff for it, its classes had to be cross-listed with other departments. Although this did not seem like the best solution, it was still important to add new cross-listed classes and to reach out to the larger community to create more visibility for the program. I set about doing that.

In 1978, before I went to graduate school, I wrote and published a book titled *I Want Somebody to Know My Name*. The publicity around the book helped create interest in and curiosity about the program, because the program got mentioned whenever I was introduced for readings or events. The *Macon Telegraph* even published a two-page spread on me and my book in the Sunday edition of the paper. It was a fabulous piece—two full pages, with lots of photographs. They talked to me about my book and my life.

I was certain most of my colleagues at Mercer had read the profile, because they all read the paper. So when I went into the office the next day, I wondered how long it would take for someone to mention the wonderful coverage. The dean of women never said a word about it, although I was sure she had read it. My office was next door to hers. The dean of students asked me if it had pleased me—but only at the end of the day, when I went into his office for another matter. No one else ever said a word about it.

The dean of women, who had provided me with some edits on the manuscript, became the most difficult person to deal with as I tried to work book promotion into my full schedule. I was very careful about how I used my time, but academics are expected to write, and I had both the faculty and administrator roles, so it was a little complicated. My schedule was packed, and I was trying to fit book promotion into any spare moment, with no institutional support from Mercer.

In these subtle ways, my colleagues at Mercer communicated the fact that they ultimately did not respect me as their peer. It seemed to me that this was because I was African American, as they did not treat any white colleagues this way. In the past, I would have suffered this treatment in silence. I would have been happy to accept any crumb of support they had to offer. But I was beginning to find my voice, so I simply told them what I would be doing to take time for myself and promote my book. I made sure I was within my contractual rights and not abusing any privilege. Instead of my appeasing them, they had to be willing to work with me. They finally had to settle into the fact that I wrote the book and it was out in the world. They wanted me to be invisible to the world, as I was invisible to them. However, I was starting to make sure that the world could see me.

Graduate school helped me to gain more of a sense of my self-worth and a voice that might be the one I could finally claim. I was very happy to be on the Atlanta University campus. For a few years before, I had chastised myself a little for not going to teach in one of the Historically Black Colleges or Universities (HBCUs). But I was learning to honor the messages that helped to direct my life. I had not felt any specific call to pursue a job in an HBCU, but getting a degree from one was exciting and what seemed like the right thing for me.

I was becoming more self-assured and grounded, so I trusted the internal messages that led me away from seeking a position at an HBCU. Instead, I chose to accept that I was in the place intended for me as I continued to pursue my academic career. Being in graduate school at Atlanta University was one of the many signs that I was on the right path. Whenever I stepped onto campus, I felt like I was exactly where I needed to be. One factor that contributed to my joy of being on the campus was my awareness that W. E. B. Du Bois had been there. I would imagine myself walking in places that he had walked and sitting in library chairs where he might have sat. It helped me to feel inspired. Du Bois could have spent time where I was on any given day.

Not everything on the Atlanta University campus was idyllic, though. For one thing, I had one professor who seemed to have a grudge against me from day one. She would not call on me to speak in class even though I would raise my hand. She made negative comments about most things I would say during class. I had never seen her before enrolling in her class. She did know that I had written a book, so perhaps she was threatened by me. But this was a graduate class, and folks come back to school after they have done an array of things. So it should not have been a surprise that I was a writer. Then she learned that I was in academia and that I was working and going to school. These were no secrets, and I saw no need to be less than open about myself. While being in that class with the professor's perplexing disdain was not pleasant, I managed to make a B in the class. I was a person on a mission. I was connected to a larger sense of purpose that pushed me past any petty conflicts or intimidations. I needed to get my graduate work done and finish my degree, so I marched on.

The most challenging part of the entire MSW program was my internship at Grady Hospital in the oncology unit. I chose that placement so that it would force me to deal with death in a more intentional manner. I thought back to the death that had overshadowed my youth. I'd been constantly aware of my half brother Garland's death through my father's stories. The terror of Emmett Till's murder had been fixed in my consciousness, even though I didn't fully understand it. After these early experiences, my father's death was devastating. Despite my resolve to face my fears, working at the Grady Hospital oncology unit turned out to be much harder than I had imagined. I had to get used to being in a hospital and around folks who were sick and dying. Along with that, I got permission to work twelve-hour days Sunday through Thursday so that I could have Fridays off to return to Macon for a class I was teaching. I went to the hospital cafeteria to eat every morning at six, and then had to be on the oncology unit by seven. I worked until six each day and then spent the evening processing the day.

When I would drive home to Macon on Thursday evenings, I cried most of the way. I was exhausted. I spent a lot of time crying during those internship months. I went to many funerals. I walked alongside many folks, and most of them died. Occasionally someone went into remission, but this was rare. Most of the time I was saying goodbye to the patients and helping their loved ones manage death. Many of our patients were indigent. Because I was there as a social worker, I had to assist with finding resources for the patients. The needed services could range from small to major. I had to find people places to live after their hospital stays, when they were too weak to work and had no home to return to. Without our intervention, these very sick people would have been living on the streets, weakened by their treatment and traumatized by their illness.

When people died, I had to find ways to fund their funerals. I wanted their lives to be celebrated; I wanted to show the world the value of their lives. I also wanted to give their families a chance to grieve properly. There was no limit to the community's needs. Our job as social workers was to do our best to meet these needs. I stayed sad during the entire length of my internship at Grady. But the time there helped me to confront death and dying in a way that I had not done before, and I am glad that I did. When I left Grady, a nurse said to me, "We are better because you were here."

Despite these struggles, I felt secure and at home in the world, especially when I was back in Macon after a hard day of work at the oncology unit. It was always wonderful to get home to my apartment. I lived in one of the larger apartments by now, which were next door to the smaller apartments I had lived in when first coming to Mercer. The larger, two- and three-bedroom apartments had small fireplaces and sun porches and big, old-fashioned bathtubs that were great for long soaks with all my herbs and oils. It was certainly paradise compared to the old nursing school dorm at Grady, where I stayed from Sunday to Thursday morning. I lived in that big drab space, which was very inexpensive because it was not really a good place for people to live. I think there were not more than two other people in the building while I was there, so it was lonely. All of this was amazingly challenging, but I knew it was going to end soon, and I had to remember to put one foot in front of the other and live one day at a time.

After completing my master's in social work, I was a bit traumatized, and it took me some time to reorganize myself. My soul had been deeply impacted by my work at Grady. I hurled myself back into my classes at Mercer, continuing to strengthen Mercer's African American studies program. I also continued engaging with students around the many needs they brought to me, both as professor and as assistant dean of women. I listened to the students' ideas about activities to pursue and created programming in response. There was a fair amount of staff changeover in the Student Life Office. Along the way, it became clear to me that I no longer wished to work with room assignments, roommate issues, complaints about beds, and all the other dorm drama.

In 1982, I stepped down as assistant dean of women and was appointed to the Mercer faculty as an instructor in and director of the African American studies program. This gave me more time to teach and to develop new classes. It was great to be able to spend more time in the academic arena, though the resources were still quite scarce. I taught several courses that were cross-listed with sociology, psychology, and literature. My favorite was "The Nature and Manifestation of Prejudice," which became a foundational course for the later work I would do around racial healing and dismantling racism. Another course was one I designed around Ida B. Wells, which was pivotal to my developing a larger consciousness about race in general and Black women in particular. This also engaged me in racial healing work, calling me to step up to the plate in new and more courageous ways.

About a year after settling into the new roles I had at Mercer, I went to speak to the president of the university, just to catch up. We had a cordial and respectful relationship. He asked me when I was going to get my PhD, and I almost fainted. I was not thinking about going back to school and was not sure I would ever want to go back. But he made a powerful case for my going back if my intentions were to stay in higher education. I listened carefully. He was basically saying that Mercer would support me in doing that if I wanted. I left his office having promised that I would think about it. I did think about it and decided I should investigate what might be possible for me to do. Again, as I had done many times before, I was saying yes to an opportunity that had presented itself.

I discovered a program at Emory University in Atlanta under what was called the Institute for the Liberal Arts. This program caught my attention because it was interdisciplinary, which meant I could combine disciplines and pursue things that I really had a deep interest in studying. When I inquired about Emory from a few folks whose opinions I respected, I was told that Emory did not graduate folks of color very well in their PhD programs. I paid no attention to that because I knew that if I applied and got accepted, I would graduate. I decided I wanted to combine Jungian psychology and African American women's literature. My work in the African American studies program at Mercer led me to focus on important Black writers, including Zora Neale Hurston and Alice Walker. I also studied African women writers, but Hurston and Walker became the primary focus of my PhD work at Emory. In my final project I used a Jungian-inspired model to work with themes of oppression and liberation in Black women writers. This, more than anything, was the work I needed to do for myself. It fed my heart's hunger. If it hadn't, I would have never been able to make it through the five years it took to earn a PhD.

I was accepted to Emory and given financial support for my tuition fees. I began the program in the summer of 1983. Mercer University granted me a leave of absence for a summer and one full academic year and continued to pay my full salary while I pursued my PhD. I lived in Atlanta for one summer and the fall and spring terms of the next school year, in order to get all my coursework and residency requirements completed. This sort of time is one of the best gifts anyone who is pursuing education can be given, because I could simply concentrate on school and not have to be working while also trying to study. Even with that gift, there were times when I felt that I was in over my head. However, I learned I was not. I just had to reimagine myself and the ways in which I studied and managed time. I developed better habits of discipline that helped me focus on my work. I learned to worry less and to work on one project or paper at a time. My first semester at Emory, I stuck to a very simple routine. I went to class, then went to the library, then went back home to study. I didn't do anything but study, write papers, and take care of the bare necessities to keep myself with clean clothes and food in the house. I do not recommend that pattern. It is not sustainable. I did well in all my classes, but it was not good for my psyche to live that way for four months.

At the end of my first semester, I was heading back home on the freeway after meeting friends for dinner and was hit by a car. This put my car into an awful spin, which finally ended with me sitting right close to the median wall. The people who hit me stopped to see if their car was all right and then took off. I had to get out of my car and make my way up an embankment to get to someone who could help me. I did that, and the police were called. It was not long before a policeman arrived. He was helpful, and when he finished the report and my undrivable car was towed away, he took me home. After that, I resolved to work less and take a few more moments to see friends or do whatever I wished. This call was too close to death, and I needed to pay attention. Although I had consistently said yes to academic opportunities, I wasn't in the habit of saying yes to the things that made me happy and made my life richer. After the car crash, I started thinking about how I could say yes to deeper friendships and more happiness in my life.

Though my self-esteem was improving, I still had a fair amount of work to do in that area. I sometimes let my denigrating inner voices cause trouble for me. When I applied for financial aid, instead of simply asking for grants so that I would have nothing to do but focus on my coursework, I asked for a grant and a teaching assistantship. I did this because I was afraid I would not be given an outright grant for the year. I was mistaken. I would have been given one. I was already an instructor at Mercer and did not need to add being a teaching assistant at Emory to the many things I had to do. There were times when I wanted to lament about this challenge that I created for myself, but I resisted that temptation and tried to pay attention to why I had put myself in that situation. I had not stood up for myself, and I had to take responsibility for making an unfortunate choice. It was a good lesson for me.

My second semester of coursework was far more difficult because I was involved with the teaching assistantship. But I managed to make it to the end. I learned to be more careful about creating hardship for myself in the future. I was able to get through, but the teaching assistantship meant I had to read about a dozen more books, none of which were helpful to my own work. It was more a distraction than anything. From this, I learned to be more discerning about the internal voices that I listened to. I learned how to recognize the voices saying that I did not deserve the opportunities I'd been presented with. I learned how to identify the choices that came from a pursuit of excellence and the choices that came from my old insecurities.

While I was in the doctoral program, I decided I needed to learn more about my African heritage, and graduate school was a perfect place to do that. Thus, I found a very good Africanist at Emory who became the chair of my dissertation committee. I also found a Jungian/Freudian and a wonderful Caribbean theologian to be on my committee. These folks were very helpful to me and led me in ways that kept my work focused. In my third year, 1983, I decided I needed to travel to West Africa. I had never been to an African country. As a matter of fact, I didn't have a passport. I had not thought much about traveling internationally until now. It is amazing how things happen. I went into my advisor's office to talk to her about the best and most affordable way to get to West Africa, and she told me about Operation Crossroads Africa, a group specializing in improving race relations by taking Black and white Americans to West Africa and the Caribbean. Each year the organization selected folks like me to lead groups of students to these places. My advisor thought I should apply.

A few days later, I went to my office at Mercer, and there was a brochure for Operation Crossroads Africa on a table near the mailboxes. I was astounded. I held it in my hand in disbelief. A week before, I had never heard of these folks, and now I stood in my office holding their brochure with all the information I needed. I could apply to become a group leader for the upcoming summer. I took the brochure home, filled it out, and sent it off. Within a month, I heard back from them. They had accepted me as a group leader, and I was invited to Princeton University for the orientation. All of us who were going to be leaders to West Africa would spend six weeks there, with four of the weeks being spent on a work project of some sort and two weeks left to travel.

The founder of Operation Crossroads Africa believed this program was an excellent way for Black and white people to learn to work together and to engage racial healing issues in an intentional manner. The idea was that both groups would benefit from being in an unfamiliar environment and sharing a common project. I was assigned to the Gambia, West Africa. They told me I was almost sent to Botswana because they thought I could handle any assignment. I have no idea why I was given that information, but I am glad I was sent to the Gambia instead. It was an assignment that would change my life on many levels.

7

The Gambia

WHEN I BEGAN MY PhD PROGRAM, I didn't really know I needed to go to Africa. I was not thinking about leaving the country for the Gambia or anywhere else. I had gotten an unexpected opportunity to go to the Middle East. The trip was sponsored by Americans for Middle Eastern Understanding and it was life changing. We went to Lebanon, Jordan, and Israel. We were in Beirut a few weeks after the Sabre and Shatila Refugee Camp massacre, which resulted in huge mass graves being erected in Beirut. I had never been in a war zone before, and the trauma of being in spaces where buildings were partially destroyed and seeing injured children who were victims of the attack on them in the refugee camp caused me great pain for many weeks and months after I returned home.

My attention was now on pursuing my degree. But after spending some time in classes exploring African culture, the hunger in my heart began to stir, and as time passed, the hunger grew. Of course, the heart hunger did not help me think about exactly where to go and how to get there. I just knew I wanted to go to West Africa. Once that was settled for me, an even bigger dilemma arose. How would I pay for it?

I had no idea. Then Operation Crossroads Africa came into my awareness. They paid all expenses, plus a three-hundred-dollar stipend for working for six weeks as a group leader. I only had to get myself to the orientation in Princeton and back home from New York when we returned from West Africa that summer. So it all came together, and I was going to the Gambia, a country that was small enough for me to learn much about, visit, and perhaps revisit someday.

When my group and I landed in Dakar, Senegal, in July 1984, we found ourselves jumping up and down, hugging each other and crying. It was very spontaneous. I was surprised by the level of emotion we felt about arriving on African soil. It was a joyous moment. I was amazed then, and as I write about it some forty years later, I am still amazed. It was as if a dam broke and our tears simply poured out of us. We were crying and rejoicing at the same time. What a sense of homecoming for us, and what affirmation for me that I needed to be on that trip. We had not really talked much about what we expected our first moments to be like. We would not have guessed how deeply personal stepping off the plane onto the ground was going to be.

I was a bit apprehensive about the trip because I was responsible for this group of young people and we were going to a place where we did not know anything except what we had been told in that brief week at Princeton. The only luggage we had was what we could carry in our backpacks. It was challenging to think of living for six weeks with so few clothes and limited necessities. But it was an opportunity like none I'd ever had before, and my heart was singing yes.

We did have someone meet us in Dakar and help us get to Banjul, Gambia. We had to take a crowded ferry to get across the river. This is one of West Africa's best waterways, but ferry navigation can be risky. Years after my group and I were there, the ferry we used was involved in accidents because they put too many people and vehicles on it. It was unsettling for us to see so many folks and cars on the ferry. I wondered how we would stay afloat, and it did cross my mind to wonder about the safety of the entire operation. We made it to Banjul and were taken to an old college where we had fairly horrible accommodations. It was made clear to us that we were living at subsistence level while there. The hotel we stayed in the first night was not that great, and it would only get worse from there. We did have some consistency, in that each place was a bit worse than the last one. At the beginning of the trip, we didn't know that the quality of many things would go down as we moved around the country.

We were going to be placed in the area called Upper River Country, in a town called Basse. It is about three hours from Banjul, the capital city. We boarded the bus that had been provided for us and made our way to Basse. When we arrived, it was already nighttime, and we had to find someone to assist us with getting our living quarters set up. We were supposed to have beds, but when we arrived, we discovered that we had only a few mattresses. We were thankful we had sleeping bags. Later, we learned that Operation Crossroads had sent money for beds to be purchased for us, but they had not been purchased. This meant that someone stole the money. They put a few mattresses at our work site, and we had to manage the entire summer without beds.

We understood that we were to experience living at the level of subsistence so that we could fully experience what is like to live like an average Gambian in the Upper River Country. However, it took a while to get used to sleeping on the concrete floor. We had to shop in the market as the local folks did, and there were many lessons to learn about food and supply shortages. At one point, the ferry could not come into the port where we were, so there was not really anything but rice in the markets. There were several days when we did not actually know where our food was to come from. We ate rice and potatoes. We were so thankful when the ferry finally arrived with bread, vegetables, and fish. We all learned many lessons about what it is like to be someplace where there is no food. And even when there is food, there is no refrigeration, so the food has to be eaten; there is no coming back for snacks or leftovers. The temperature is over one hundred degrees, and all the water has been heated by the sun. There is no ice. For me, the most profound lesson was when the water was turned off in our part of town in the middle of my attempt to take a shower, and I would have to finish the shower without water or wait until someone went to the river to get some. I usually opted to end the shower.

Our team took turns cooking. Some of the students didn't know how to cook at all because they had never had to cook before. All the students who were on this trip were middle- and upper-class young people. We never had quite enough to eat. Some of the people in the group found this life to be very taxing. At one point they demanded I take them to a hotel. Actually, I was not opposed to the idea, but the nearest hotel was five hours away back in Banjul, and we were not going to travel back there until we finished our work project. One of the participants had to leave and return home because she simply could not handle all the hardship and the uncertainty about food. There were a few times when I questioned my sanity for wanting to bring a group of well-off college students on such a trip for six weeks. They complained a lot, and some of them got sick or were not too well for the entire trip. But, out of twelve, eleven of my crew stayed to the end.

The Crossroaders worked for a couple of weeks on helping to construct a school building, and some of them chose to leave that project to work with the women in the rice fields. In the Gambia, rice is grown only by women, and it is not an easy process. The men grow groundnuts (peanuts), which is not as labor-intensive. If you managed to get up before the sun rose, you would see the farm women walking to gather firewood. They would make breakfast for their families. Then they would go to the rice fields. They work there all day and then come home to cook. Because rice is the staple food in the Gambia, there is still a need for importing a lot of it. So these rice-growing women do not get the best return on their labor because they cannot really compete with international, corporate rice growers. It was heartbreaking to see how long the days were for them and how hard they worked, while the men had much more leisure time. The men spent a lot of time sitting under baobab trees and in the evenings making really strong green tea.

Students who would choose to spend their summer on a work trip like this are already folks who are about more than the latest pair of designer jeans or making sure to be seen every minute of every day on social media. Thus, the entire summer impacted them tremendously. We were supporting people of the Gambia with education (building the school) and food supply (cultivating rice). What better ways to be helping a nation?

The women working in the wet rice fields had much trouble with leeches covering their feet and legs when they left the fields each day. They worked with bare feet and had to put oil on their legs when they finished working each day. I do not want to think about the impact this had on the women's health in the long run and the pain of it each day in the short run. No wonder the men don't grow the rice. That water where the rice grew was there as a result of the massive rainy season. It rained enough every day for us to wonder if we needed to find if there was an ark someplace that could rescue us. This is how the women were able to grow rice during the rainy season. The students who worked with them in the fields didn't find that work uplifting, and they were sympathetic toward the women and the hardships they faced.

There was not much entertainment in Basse, but we managed to find ways to keep ourselves busy. I was invited from time to time to do things with the students in some of the surrounding villages when there was drumming and dancing. Many in my group were fairly adventuresome, perhaps more than I was. So it was good for them to get out and bring back information to those of us who were not quite as outgoing.

One Sunday, the students implored me to arrange a trip on the river for them. A man came with a boat and offered to take us on this trek for a price. We bargained and finally agreed on a sum. We all piled onto his boat, along with a handful of locals. One of those locals was a person named Muhammad Njie. He did not have a lot to say to us. However, he had stepped up to help me bargain for the boat because there was concern that the boatman would try to overcharge us. Though I did not know it at the time, the boatman did overcharge us, and his boat was not safe. By the end of the day, the boatman was dipping water out of the boat because it had a hole in it. I am very aware of the amazing grace that was extended to us because we were on the Gambia River all day, which is almost like being in the ocean. It is beautiful and powerful. I am thankful to this day that I managed to get back home safely with all of my team. Despite this danger, which we weren't aware of at the time, the river was magnificent. I was very glad we had arranged to take this outing. We stopped along the way for a bit and found food, but other than that, we spent the day traveling on that beautiful waterway. The Gambia River is a major waterway in West Africa. When the British and French were stealing land from the native people who lived there, the British wanted the river and the small amount of land on either side of it.

That is why the country is called the Gambia—because it is named for the river. The French took Senegal. I spent as much time as I could there on the river, and each trip back to the Gambia always finds me more excited about the river than anything else.

I fell in love with the Gambia River. But what I slowly realized was that I was also falling in love with Muhammad Njie, or Modou, the beautiful African prince in my eyes, who had negotiated the price of our passage. He carried my satchel all day and took some responsibility to make sure the day went well for this strange group of Americans. I was impressed by his presence and his engagement with us. We talked a little about the river and the country, but we didn't talk that much. It was easier to simply take in the day without too many words. He had an aura of confidence and clarity about how to manage the parts of the day that needed managing, and while I am usually quite good at that myself, I was glad for him to help us that day.

By the time we got back to our quarters, it seemed as if we had been gone for a week. We were all wiped out. It turned out that Modou, the man who had been so solicitous on the boat, worked at the bank in Basse. He wanted to continue our conversations, so over the next few weeks, he would come to our compound after dinner and go for walks with me before the sun went down. (Folks don't go out walking after dark due to their concern about hyenas.) It was great talking to him. He was so knowledgeable about West Africa and many other parts of the world. We talked for hours. We were able to get food at the little eatery in Basse, and there was often a party that we went to while I was there. But our time was coming to a rapid close.

We knew we wanted to see each other again before I returned to the US, but my group and I were heading to Dakar for two weeks, and Modou was in Basse. So it seemed unlikely because it was not that simple to travel. But when the universe is involved in orchestrating, many amazing things can and will happen. We parted ways, and we didn't have cell phones or even landlines to be calling to make arrangements. Our group left as scheduled for Dakar. I told Modou where we would be, but I didn't have much hope that our paths would actually cross again. Modou wasn't sure he could get away from the bank long enough to come to Senegal because that would take two to three days of traveling back and forth.

My very practical left side of my brain told me it made no sense to be falling in love with a man who lived halfway around the world from me, in this small village that didn't really have decent telephone service, and where it took weeks to get mail delivered. But I was not in charge of this amazing happening that my heart was managing as I was being transformed by falling in love with the Continent, with Modou, and with my ancestral heritage. I had no idea that all of these changes would come to my head and heart from taking a cohort of young students to West Africa. I was in the land of my ancestors, and I had been given such an openhearted welcome at the airport by the ancestors. The whole time I was there, many folks would say to me, "Welcome home, Sister." And I had come to the conclusion a long time before this trip that most of the men I crossed paths with in the US were afraid of me because I was smart, clearheaded, and really focused on what I was searching for on this earth. American men were intimidated by my fierce intention to find the path to whatever was meant for me and to freedom. So the man who was open to a relationship with such a woman as I happened to be was somewhere else. At least, that was my conclusion. It seems I was right. It is amazing that Modou and I just might have found one another on a leaky boat on the Gambia River on a hot summer day in July.

At any rate, I loved Modou Njie. And if I didn't ever see him again, I was really glad our paths had crossed. But I hoped he might show up in Dakar. Dakar is amazing—so different from Banjul. There are restaurants, shops, and street vendors with almost every imaginable ware you could think of, ready to bargain with you so that you will finally decide the deal is just too good to pass up, whether you need what is being sold or not. I loved watching the beautiful folks in both the Gambia and Senegal. I will never forget the delight that filled my heart to see the women in their Sunday attire. I just wanted to take a seat on the sidewalk and watch them go about their business of the day. Of course, everyone was speaking Wolof or some other African language in both countries. I had a hard time catching on to speak Wolof, and my French never got beyond classroom speaking, but I managed to shop and to order food and to conduct the hotel business for our group.

We were in Dakar for six days and then went to the Senegalese island city of Saint-Louis, which is a few hours from Dakar. The main attraction there is the slave holding pens and the Gate of No Return. These structures were placed on the edge of the sea so that the slave ship could pull up to the doors of the holding pens, where enslaved Africans were being kept like caged animals, and load its human "cargo." It is not a pleasant place to visit. It was a stark contrast from the stone circles we had visited in the Gambia. The Senegambian stone circles are much like the stone circles in northwestern Europe. It is not known who brought them here, but the place in which they're erected is clearly a holy place. The energy and the air in that space is not the same as in the rest of the country. And come to think of it, neither is the energy and the air around Saint-Louis—for a very different set of reasons. The Gate of No Return tells a different story. Even without knowing the exact history of the stone circles, clearly one story is about life and the other one is about death.

Saint-Louis is a beautiful enough place, but the slave trade tainted its soul in ways that all sites where dehumanization occurred are tainted. We stayed there for three days and then headed back to Dakar for the remainder of our time. My team loved that we were traveling, and we spent a great deal of our time on the way back to Dakar trying to imagine how we would stay in touch with one another.

When we got back to Dakar, I tried to get in touch with Modou, but the phone service was too squirrely, and I had to simply let the idea of arranging to meet again go by the wayside. So, I did. On our final day, we went on our last outing, and when we got back to our hotel, Modou was there waiting for us. I couldn't believe he got off from work and that he found us. I was delighted. My team was glad as well. So we got a chance to be in beautiful Dakar together before departing for the airport the next morning. He promised he would come to the States if we could work out all the details. I was not about to hold on to that hope because it seemed beyond possible. But I know better than to limit God, the angels, the ancestors, and all the heavenly host. So we began a transcontinental courtship that consisted of letter writing and sporadic phone calls until the next summer.

That summer, I went back to the Gambia on my own, spending the summer with Modou and his family. I stayed in the Gambia the entire time, and I had a chance to visit the river a lot. I also sat in small restaurants and listened to folks speak Wolof, still picking up only a little of the language. I did become a consummate bargainer, though. Modou and his family talked about going to the shops with me because they didn't want me to get cheated. But when I would come back and tell them what I bought and what I paid for it, they teased me that they should have been worrying for the shop owners instead of me. It was a glorious summer, and I really hated to leave to return to Macon and my fall teaching schedule and dissertation writing, but I did. However, Modou promised he would come in the late fall or early winter.

Frankly, I still didn't understand projection as well as I do now—not that understanding it would have changed much about this relationship. But understanding projection more fully at the time might have helped me to stay a little bit more connected to how complicated my relationship with Modou really was. I was this well-established college professor falling in love with a man ten years younger than me, who had not finished college yet. What did we think would come of this connection? We didn't know, and for the most part, we just kept going forward and not asking too many questions. But our cultural differences would clash at some point. A little more tempering of all that was happening with a hearty dose of reality would have been helpful.

Some of my friends thought I was not being smart. Others who knew me better were beaming with joy for me as they watched new parts of me come to life and witnessed the joy I had when Modou finally arrived in the States and we decided to get married. It had been just over one year since that leaky boat ride on the Gambia River. It was a good day for me, and I don't regret one moment of this part of my journey. I learned how to dance better, how to play more. I experienced how much fun it was to go to see two or three movies in one day and find food in between and stay up late talking about the movies. It was sheer joy for Modou to see a movie the day it opened in theaters because in the Gambia, he was used to having to wait for months for new movies to become available. So these things that I took for granted were good to see through the eyes of someone who deeply appreciated and enjoyed them in a way I never had before.

After we got married in 1985, Modou enrolled in college to finish his bachelor's degree in English, while I was finishing my PhD. I was proud to have finally connected to a man who was not afraid of me and who was willing to trust his own sense of self enough to be this committed to a woman who was older and more educated. It was good to get beyond some of the externals that are not essential to loving another person. It isn't simple, because life is complicated, and we had merged cultural differences, religious differences, and many other differences. But both of us decided not to make them a problem until they became a problem. It took a while for them to begin to be challenging.

I think that life is lived in seasons. We had a season of domestic harmony. Modou had a young son in the Gambia, and he wanted his son to live with us so that the child could have a better life. I was quite all right with that. But just as I was taking preliminary exams for my PhD, I discovered I was pregnant. I was quite all right with that as well, but my body was not as happy about it as my heart was. I had severe headaches every day for quite some time, and there is nothing like trying to write your doctoral preliminary exams with splitting migraines. I found little windows where I could write, and I worked really hard on the questions, and while I am not exactly sure how I did it, I managed to finish them, and more importantly, I managed to pass. It is all a blur in my mind at this point. Following the completion of my exams and my moving to candidacy status, Modou's son, Mbye, arrived to live with us. I gave birth to William in March 1986, and Modou graduated from Mercer. I was still writing my dissertation and would graduate in 1987.

I enjoyed being a wife, mother, professor, and student. But it was too much. In my effort to manage everything, I became ill with rheumatoid arthritis and fibromyalgia. Life became extremely stressful. The days of going to see two or three movies a day and then out to dinner were gone. They were replaced with emergency room visits to treat the extreme attacks of joint pain I began to have. We also had to manage the lives of busy schoolchildren and our jobs, including all the preparation I had to do in order to teach a few new classes from time to time. Modou got a teaching job and had his own sets of papers and preparation for classes to manage. The onset of rheumatoid arthritis was a major disruption in our lives. I tried really hard to keep doing everything I had been doing, but it became impossible. I went to soccer games, school activities for the children, and a few work-related events at Mercer when I had to. The work of managing a chronic illness is unbelievably demanding. Our entire family suffered with me because of this illness.

Rheumatoid arthritis became my teacher. I learned so much about self-care that I might not have pursued if I had never experienced this illness. I learned about nutrition. I began acupuncture and massage. Along with this, I learned to handle stress in a different way. In addition, I learned to practice silence more. I continued to work with good psychotherapists who helped me as well. I learned about herbal therapies and finally found an amazing integrative medicine practitioner who had trained with Dr. Andrew Weil, the master of integrative medicine. She was a great companion on the journey toward getting better. As time passed, I engaged herbalists, various physicians, massage therapists, acupuncturists, integrative medicine practitioners, people at St. Francis Episcopal Church (who prayed daily for me), journal keeping, gallons of essential oils, Epsom salt, all kinds of creams and salves, a few prescription drugs, a plant-based diet, and the removal of all processed food from my diet. I developed all the new stress management techniques I could and found aquatic exercise routines. I spent so much time doing all this while still taking care of my work and home responsibilities.

It was an uphill journey fraught with much pain and dis-appointment as well as depression, but I stayed the course. I remained open to the lessons of rheumatoid arthritis, just as I had stayed open to all the previous lessons of my life. Strange as it was, I found myself saying yes to this experi-ence, just as I'd always done before. I knew I had to work on this illness in many ways and that it was going to take all the energy and determination I could find to get better. During this time, my mother died, and it felt as if the earth moved and there was not any stable ground to stand on. Then Mo-dou's father died and he had to go back to the Gambia. All of this was simply additional layers of stress and sadness to manage. But the work was clearly laid out for me, and I was determined to stay faithful.

During all this effort, there was only one question to answer: Do you want to be well? My answer was yes. I was willing to do whatever it takes to be well—at least I was on most days. There were days when I was simply sick and tired of being sick and tired, and I know my family was tired of it also. I remember that when I quit eating meat, Mbye was appalled and worried that I would not be able to survive. He asked me with a look of horror on his face, "Are you never going to eat meat again?"

As a result of all the focused work I did, I was healed of fi-bromyalgia. I am so thankful for that healing process, because I think the fibromyalgia contributed to my constant pain even more than the rheumatoid arthritis. While my rheumatoid arthritis had pain associated with it, the type of total body pain I experienced was gone. I still have rheumatoid arthritis, so I've concluded that my worst pain was more than likely related to fibromyalgia. A part of my challenge was to learn how to see myself as being more than a person who was limited by an illness. I had to work on seeing myself as capable, even though there were many things I could no longer do. I had to factor my illness into many decisions, but that did not make me less of a person. My self-concept was significantly challenged, and I learned a lot about reimagining myself. I was able to find new things that could be celebrated. This tutorial has been long. The diagnosis came when I was thirty-eight years old and today, over thirty years later, I'm still dealing with rheumatoid arthritis. It continues to be my teacher and guide; I am still learning its lessons. Every day I must continue in my intentional self-care practices. My teacher keeps me vigilant, and I am reminded to not lose focus on nutrition, therapy, integrative medicine, herbal healing, massage, acupuncture, small amounts of prescription drugs, and prayer. These lessons, although of great value, came alongside great loss.

This season was very challenging. The stress of rheumatoid arthritis took an enormous toll. A significant casualty was my marriage. Modou thought I should declare myself disabled and quit teaching. I was in really terrible shape during those earlier years with RA. Perhaps I could have taken a few more prescription medicines, but when I was told all the side effects, I determined that they were worse than the illness itself. Many of the medicines could even result in death, which rheumatoid arthritis would not, so I decided against them.

I still grieve the loss of Modou and the love we shared. I grieve the loss of the early part of our being married and the fact that we did not get to a place that could provide a container for the next season, which was so painful. But it was a good part of the journey, and I do not lament that season. It was bitter and sweet and I learned a lot. Furthermore, I have two of the best men anyone could ask for in my sons, Mbye and William. They are gifts, and I will be grateful into eternity for them and for the good journey we have had and continue to have together.

Modou left us in Macon and moved to Atlanta. I was not in any shape to relocate, so we both knew that was not going to happen. The more we tried to make ourselves believe otherwise, the more we decided we needed to go our own separate ways. So I took it upon myself to file the divorce paperwork. I think it would have been harder for Modou to get it done because he kept thinking we might find a remedy somewhere—but there was not any space for looking for remedies. The only remedy was to wish each other the best and move on with our lives. We have both done that, and life is good for our sons and me. I do not see Modou much, but he lives outside the US and I think he is all right. I hope he is and that he finds all that will make his life what he wants it to be.

As I think about the impact of my time in the Gambia on my psychological and spiritual development, I continue to be amazed. I didn't know how central Africa was to my search for freedom. Even though there was pain and loss associated with the awakening that came from being engaged by the spirit of Africa, I will always be grateful that I had the opportunity to be enriched by that spirit. I understand some of the reasons why this experience—standing on the soil of the continent of Africa, being in conversation with the Gambia River, falling in love with one of Africa's sons, and having a chance to shepherd my young sons who embody the DNA of Africa—has helped me in my quest for personal freedom. But there is still much to learn about this time in my life. I will continue to listen in order to hear more about how I am to feel and embrace the spirit of Africa in my life as I continue to seek to be a faithful pilgrim.

So, after twelve years of being married, I was single again. However, I now had my two wonderful sons to accompany me on the way and the deep awakening of parts of my soul that were delighted to see the light. My sons were eight and thirteen when Modou and I divorced. I was fearful about becoming a single mother in America. My early years had made me accustomed to living with unnamed fear. But now I could name the fears I was facing: economic precarity, white supremacy's violence, aloneness, raising Black boys without their father, and my own health struggles. But my new sense of empowerment allowed me to listen to sounds other than the numbing sound of fear. My experience taught me that I could always be open to whatever life had to offer me. I had learned more about how to dance to the music that was being played. This was certainly not the time to put my hands over my ears and complain, though at times I wondered who was selecting the music. I was grieving for the death of my relationship with my African prince. But I was also really scared about being alone, trying to raise these boys in this country that did not have their best interests at its forefront. I did not have enough money. I was not well due to my struggle with RA. All the negative statistics kept rolling through my head about Black boys being raised by single mothers.

These thoughts filled me with fear regarding what was ahead for my sons as we tried to make our way through the world without their father. The thought of being a single black mother raising sons was earth-shattering. However, my children had to see me stepping up to the plate to do whatever was needed. They did not deserve to have their father leave and their mother fall apart, so I did not fall apart. Although it was a desperate situation, I had already learned how to say yes to life, rather than giving in to the voice of desperation. So I continued this practice and said yes to this daunting situation.

I gave my oldest son, Mbye, a choice to go live with his father because he was not my birth son and I didn't want him to feel trapped in a place where he didn't want to be. He chose to stay with me and his brother. I was so glad. I wanted to take my sons and leave the United States. However, I didn't know where we could actually go, and clearly, our support systems were here. It would have made no sense to leave. So we persevered. We were in the habit of surviving, and that is what we kept on doing.

I told my sons that there were big, strong angels standing at the end of the driveway to make sure we were all right. I wasn't sure if they were there or not, but I had a deep sense of being protected. I believed that my sons and I were going to be all right in spite of my fear and trembling, and I wanted them to feel safe and secure. I read the Ninety-First Psalm every day for a year. I was so taken by the psalmist's declaration of God loving us like a mother and being covered under God's wings. One day, as I was meditating on the psalm, a mother bird came and built her nest in a flowerpot on our front porch. I didn't know the little bird family was there until I observed the mother flying back and forth with food for her babies. When I went out to investigate, I found them. It was such lovely affirmation. I was very thankful. I felt like I was holding on to a rope that disappeared into a deep, dark cave. I was holding on to the very end of the rope, but I was still holding on. Messages, like the image of the mother bird, came to me periodically. They were like knots tied in the rope. Each knot helped me continue holding on. And they helped me navigate a way forward, even in the darkness.

Of course I worried about my sons. But they were the best. They worked hard. They helped me by doing what they needed to do. I will always be grateful to them for this. They didn't take detours from staying focused in school. They didn't get sidetracked. They are very fine young men. I am grateful each day for their presence in my life and in the world. My life and the world are improved by their being here. I am glad I had the honor of shepherding them to this point. I said yes to parenting them, despite great hardship, and they consistently answered me with their own yes to being the best sons possible.

8

Witness

DESPITE MY HARDSHIPS, I CONTINUED to stay on an academic career path that made sense to me. As a result, my work became more visible. The African American studies program at Mercer grew. We picked up majors, and it was beginning to look as if we might be able to move it to a bit more of a prominent space within the undergraduate curriculum. Earning my PhD gave me a new status among my faculty peers. They were not concerned about the focus of it; their concern was more about my having earned it, which gave me a better right to be with them as an equal. Nothing had ever been said *to* me about my status, but I had heard conversations about others that made me aware that there were more than likely similar things being said *about* me before I finished my PhD.

The lack of institutional commitment to African American studies from the university caused me to look for ways to connect our work in the university to the community in Macon. It was important for the community at large to know about the university's efforts, small and stingy though they were, to ensure the equity and inclusion of African American culture and history. And if people in the community

knew more about the program, they would have more opportunities to speak out in support of it. In 1996, I said yes to one
of the most important projects of my entire academic career,
although at the time it seemed like I was merely addressing a crisis. During Black History Month, I was supposed to
present one speaker who would use their celebrity to bridge
the wide chasm that existed between Black folks and white
America. However, I was not prepared to find that person in
the time frame I had available to me. So instead of seeking
out a celebrity, I decided we needed to honor Black women
from the Macon area, beginning with twenty-five in this first
year. I had a vision of a four-year campaign that would eventually bring one hundred Black women to the table. Then in
the fifth year, after we had celebrated four groups of twenty-
five, we would have an event that would bring all one hundred women together for a larger celebration.

The dean liked the idea, and we moved forward with it. It
was called the Standing on Their Shoulders Project. It was a
delight getting folks nominated by people in their respective
communities, letting them know of their nominations and
requesting their short biographies. The stories were so rich.
These women were the ordinary faithful ones who keep on
dancing to the music that's playing, no matter how difficult
the dance becomes. Once I received their bios, if I needed
more information, I had the pleasure of traveling to many of
their homes to gather it. Once I had collected all the information I needed, my student helpers and I put together a mono-
graph with the women's photographs and bios included. We
hosted a luncheon for them, and then we had a public program that was open to the community. Each woman was
presented by a local middle or high school student and was
celebrated by the community in the reception to follow. The
Macon Telegraph covered the project, publishing photos of
and write-ups on each woman. It was good for the African

American studies program to host such events because no one had ever done anything like this before. Many of these women had never had anyone acknowledge them and the lives they had lived as people dedicated to service. One of them ran a breakfast program out of her own kitchen. She would stand in her front doorway and ask schoolchildren who were passing by her house if they had eaten breakfast; if they had not, she gave them breakfast. Another one of the women decided she wanted to be a high school graduate and began to take GED classes. She was a faithful student who got her high school diploma when she was sixty-five years old. All of us who had a chance to go to school, and to have a better life than our foremothers, were standing on our fore-mothers' shoulders. These women needed to know we understood that—and that we wanted to honor them. They were so humbled by this program, and the community seemed filled with gratitude about it.

We ran the program for four years, as I intended. Then we got support from the local Tubman African American Museum to publish a coffee-table book recognizing all the women. Each woman had a full-page spread with her photo and biographical information, and they were all invited to the Tubman for a massive autographing session. We had a large group portrait made by Horace Holmes Photography Studio, who had taken all the individual photos for the book. Afterward, he donated the large photo to us.

It took nine years to go from the first Standing on Their Shoulders session to the celebration of all one hundred women. But it was years well spent. This might be the most powerful portion of the public work I did in Macon. I think it was the elevation of the everyday heroines that made it so wonderful. These women got up each day and went about their daily responsibilities. They had limited time, but they always made time to include others. They weren't worried about being inconvenienced. They were servants. I was so honored to be involved with them as we put this project together and shared it with others. We heard of a few people replicating our idea in their own communities.

In 2018, a wonderful woman approached me about spotlighting one more group of women for the Standing on Their Shoulders Project. I was reluctant because she insisted that I be included and I was not sure how I felt about that, but she was clearly determined. After several conversations, I said yes. We identified a group of fifteen additional women to be celebrated. I was quite surprised at the memory folks had about the project, as it had been thirteen years since our last event. Even though we didn't get to do all the publicity I would have wished, we had a packed house. There is something about celebrating folks in the community that captures people's imaginations and inspires. As a result, people simply keep showing up for anything related to Standing on Their Shoulders: Celebrating the Wisdom of African American Women. I'm glad the dean gave me the opportunity to think more creatively about celebrating Black History Month and that I listened to my head and heart, which led me to this project that has kept being a light in the community—and in other communities as well.

This program helped to enlarge my voice in Macon. I began to write for the *Macon Telegraph*. For eleven years, I wrote a biweekly column covering many topics. I received a lot of backlash from white men and some white women who were just unable to believe I should have the space and freedom to say whatever I wanted to say about things like race, class, gender, ableism, ageism, violence, and guns. Some of them went to the publisher, trying to get him to stop me from writing. One person at Mercer thought he was going to get me to write the things he thought I should be writing. He was a white man who didn't want me to talk about the issues I deemed important. He believed he could tell me what to write because he was a white man; I thought his ego was making him think far more of himself than he should have. I had no intention of concerning myself with him and his racist and sexist notions. I tried to simply listen to his side of an issue while still telling the truth as I knew it. When he realized this, he changed his strategy. He went around Macon trying to get people who had invited me to speak to disinvite me. However, people knew I was speaking the truth, though there were those who were trying, to no avail, to get me silenced as a columnist. The man who was trying to convince me to quit writing what I wanted to write finally gave up on trying to manage me and my voice.

Mercer was a good place for me to sharpen my voice. As I grew in confidence about the things I found to be important, I had a platform from which to speak. I began to be called by news stations when they wanted someone to comment about a social justice issue or race or abuse. I was often asked to make a comment on extrajudicial killings by police, gang violence, or racist acts against people of color. I was finding my voice and was courageous enough to use it to speak out about many things. In some ways this felt a bit strange. I watched myself arrive in this space and remembered how much silence I had lived with in my own head and heart as a younger person. Growing up, I didn't know how to articulate a lot of things, and I was not always sure what I thought about things either. The world felt uncontrollable, like the Arkansas storms, or unknowable, like the highway shrouded in mist, which I had found so frightening as a child.

But my clarity and courage began to get stronger and stronger. I could feel myself ready to stand my ground on issues like reports of abuses of prisoners, Black-on-Black crime, homelessness, and other justice issues. I could speak as forcefully as possible at every opportunity that was afforded me. I had come quite a distance since my childhood. Even as an undergraduate, facing the murder of Larry Kimmons, and as a graduate student, trying to make sense of death, my voice was still developing. But now I was beginning to believe I had a right to say whatever I chose to say whenever I might choose to say it. It was liberating. It gave me a reason to hope I would continue finding the answers to some of the many questions I had about the way life unfolds. It might've been easy to give in to fear, but instead, I made the daily decision to say yes. After all, saying yes had put me on this path before I ever had any idea of where it would be going. So now that I had a clearer idea of what my path was, I had an even clearer idea of what I was saying yes to, and how I might continue the process of saying yes.

One day, in 1999, my phone rang before 8:00 a.m., and when I answered it, the voice of Dr. R. Kirby Godsey, the president of Mercer, startled me. Though I enjoyed a cordial relationship with him, I could not recall him having ever called me at home before. I couldn't imagine what he wanted that couldn't wait until the workday actually began. However, I was glad to speak to him because conversations with him were always encouraging and pleasant.

This morning's conversation was full of surprises. He wondered if I would be interested in becoming a loaned executive to the Macon mayor, Jim Marshall, who was a member of the Mercer Law School faculty. If so, I would be released from all my teaching duties but would continue to receive full salary. I would run the mayor's Youth Violence Prevention Task Force because the city was having multiple homicides a week. I would report to city hall every day instead of to my campus office. I was speechless. I was fascinated. I was glad.

There was no way to know how challenging the work would be. I had no way to even begin to imagine anything about it because I had no idea what would be involved. I didn't really know the mayor, even though he was a colleague of sorts in the Mercer Law School. When I went to meet him, it was clear he was a no-nonsense person and that he wanted results, which is what he told me. It was an awkward meeting with him and his chief of staff. They both seemed rather starched and ironed, which was not the type of person I was accustomed to working with. But they seemed fine with me. We agreed that I would begin in May 1997, as soon as the current school term ended, which meant I would be working in the summer instead of teaching summer school and preparing for the new school year.

The challenges began at the very beginning. The mayor and his chief of staff offered me what amounted to mostly a broom closet for an office, and I said absolutely not. I am not sure what they were thinking. I knew they had to find a suitable workspace for me. If they were to treat this program as a priority, they had to show that through finding space for it. I told them both that I would work in my office at Mercer until they found a space. The mayor said he wanted me on the premises, and I told him to let me know when he had a suitable space for me to use. I went home after that conversation and was a bit surprised by my clarity and courage in simply stating what was required for me to begin a satisfactory journey with them. My sense of self and the voice that was developing with it were becoming more evident to me. I was not intimidated by the mayor's social standing; after all, he was the one who had been seeking my assistance, not the other way around. Though I was a bit worried he might take the appointment back, I knew I was not going to work each day from a broom closet. By this time, I was able to see my worth and speak the truth of that worth. I worked from my Mercer office for a few days. When I had resigned myself to the fact that my remedy might be indefinite, I got a phone call informing me that they had found an office for me. They created another problem for themselves by displacing another person, an African American woman contractor, who was quite upset about being moved. It seems significant that, in order to make space for me, another Black woman had to lose her space. While I was sorry about the confusion, it was not my issue to resolve, and I managed to steer fairly clear of it.

The mayor appointed his Youth Violence Prevention Task Force to address the growing gang violence issue in Macon. It was also intended to address the disenfranchisement of young Black and brown folks. The summer I began that work, there were thirty homicides in Macon. This was a significant jolt for a town with a population under 150,000. Of course, there were many voices who felt they had the answer to the problems facing us. It was our job to discern between these various voices, differentiating the unhelpful from the helpful. While much of the input was not helpful, there was one idea from a Bibb County art teacher about using mural painting to help combat the proliferation of gang graffiti around the city. I researched this idea and found that many folks were having good success with that around the country. While it is not easy to assess the effectiveness of such initiatives, in the case of murals, it was easy. The gangs did not as a general rule return to reconstruct their graffiti after it was painted over.

The city officials, parents, teachers, and others who cared about children and their welfare were glad our task force decided to take on this idea and begin a Saturday mural-painting initiative. It was a phenomenal success. For one thing, the youngsters who became involved were delighted to be asked to help in this manner. Along with that, they had a chance to design what they painted with a bit of guidance from their art teacher. There were many folks in the city who stepped up to provide funds for supplies and lunches. The groups painted murals in several parks and recreational centers because those were always the first places that got the full-blown treatment of the gang graffiti. We did this work more than twenty years ago, and those places that have murals were never the recipient of gang graffiti ever again. It was remarkable. Our hearts were encouraged by the immediate response, and the longevity continues to be hard to believe.

The task force sponsored the mural project, and because it was so successful, we received many invitations to speak about it in the media. There were times when I thought we talked about our work too much because our children were still killing one another, and we were a long way from finding any remedies for the violence. Nonetheless, we talked about the work, and we raised enough money to paint a lot of park walls across Macon.

Along with painting murals, we engaged in gun buybacks, which were quite popular during the early 1990s in an effort to combat gang violence. We gave anyone who brought in any type of working gun fifty dollars and asked no questions. I was so thankful for the cooperative spirit and counsel of the chief of police. He helped me work out the plan for the gun buybacks and provided officers to be present each time we hosted those sessions. We also had many citizens give us donations to help pay for the guns. We bought many guns during that season, and once we bought them, the police department helped us with discarding them. The chief of police always asserted that every gun we got was one less gun on the streets. Although the work was effective, it could be heartbreaking at times. One morning, during a buyback session, two boys showed up who looked to be about eleven or twelve years old. Both of them came with small handguns to turn in. I looked at them and could see how young they were. It broke my heart for them to be standing in front of me, waiting to see how much money they could realize by handing over these means of death that appeared to be keeping them safe. These two little boys came over to me and gave me a hug when we gave them their money in exchange for the guns. I was in tears. They were also. I wondered what on earth we had done to construct our world such that our children found themselves in this very dangerous position of trying to navigate their lives by owning guns when they were still in elementary school. While I didn't know exactly the path our society had taken to get to this place where our children believed that they needed guns to help them live each day, at least we were catching glimpses of a few ways to get onto another path.

The mayor's task force also hosted youth-oriented programs on violence involving the Macon Museum of Arts and Sciences and Macon's medical communities. One of our best programs was an art exhibition that emerged from a day of conversations between emergency room doctors and school-children from across the region. The exhibition focused on gun violence, and we invited emergency room doctors and other health-care professionals to come talk to middle and high school students about violence and violence prevention. We had these sessions divided into two-hour segments so that we could accommodate as many students as possible. That system worked well, allowing us to have close to three hundred students attend the program for that day.

Along with these programs, we organized events for adults, bringing prominent leaders in the youth violence prevention arena to assist us. All these programs and initiatives required me to speak to the media a great deal, which continued to support my journey toward finding my voice. I had to be consistent and brave in naming the issues the community was facing. And I also had to speak the truth regardless of whether that truth was popular with the people listening.

All the work I did while serving as a loaned executive for what turned into two years was transformative for me, but the portion that had the greatest impact was the work I did with parents, mostly mothers, who had lost their children to gun violence. We organized a couple of fairly extensive marches against violence. The leaders of these marches were the grieving parents who called themselves the Mourning Mothers. One of our community partners drew a beautiful picture of a grieving mother. We used the image as a background for some of our publicity, and the name emerged from that vision. The women brought creativity and great passion to the work. All of them had lost a child to gun violence, and several of them had lost more than one.

One major project was the creation of a quilt of remembrance. We engaged a local artist to assist us in designing and creating the quilt that included photographs of the community's murdered children. For all of us, it was very difficult to complete this project. We worked on it at city hall, in the mayor's large conference room. We brought all the materials into that space and met there each week until we finished the project. I'm sure that nothing like that had ever been done there before or since. It was good for all of us. I remember one of the mothers whose entire family had been murdered; she was the person who had come home and found them. One day, she had a complete meltdown and threw all the materials that she was working with in the trash and left the room. She simply could not stand it anymore. One of the other mothers got up quietly from her chair and went to the trash and collected everything and neatly put it away. She knew this space that we had created was one that would bring the brokenhearted mother back at some point. Despite her pain, she would be sorry she had thrown her materials away. This proved to be true. A few days later she returned, and we all helped her get back to her work of making a fitting memorial for her family.

We laughed and cried a lot while we made the quilt. There were about thirty women working together on it and a total of forty or more homicidal deaths of their children within that one small group. We had to cry, but weeping does end at some point and light or joy comes. We had a few such moments. When we finally finished the quilt, we had a major event surrounding its hanging in the lobby of city hall. It stayed there during my two years and a bit beyond but was finally moved to the Macon convention center. It may have been discarded in later years because there were many complaints about it being morbid. However, all of us who worked on helping to construct it had found that it helped us to imagine new possibilities for addressing the violence and death that was hounding us. It was good to have this concrete product to see at the end of our lamenting together.

The season of serving as a loaned executive helped me to better solidify what it means to be a witness. It moved me toward learning what it means to have a prophetic voice. Once I read a wonderful poem that included lines about speaking for the voiceless. The person who is given the opportunity to see injustice and to find ways to address it must speak for the ones who cannot or will not speak for themselves. It takes courage and integrity to be a witness and to speak about has been seen or heard.

Along with my other initiatives, I called together some of the major religious leaders in the city, at the mayor's request, to implore them to help provide leadership against gang violence. Unfortunately, most of them were preoccupied with finding grant support for themselves and seemed rather void of good, concrete ideas. They didn't seem to have much energy to bring to the table if they were not going to receive funding for whatever efforts they imagined. This was during the era of the Clinton administration's Weed and Seed initiative to clean up neighborhoods fraught with crime, unemployment, and all the other factors that were unsupportive of empowered living. But Weed and Seed was not working. There was too much need, and the help was far too little and much too late. The program had good intentions, but it didn't have enough wraparound services. It was not sustainable long enough to provide what so many youngsters—who had sought the gangs because they were seeking a family—needed to find their way to a more stable life.

But many of the religious leaders in the Weed and Seed neighborhoods were sure they should get money to help their congregations. After they got the money, they would think of what they might do for others in the community. For example, in one of our most devastated neighborhoods, funding from the Weed and Seed program resulted in an old storefront being brightly painted and filled with computers. But drug use and gang activity continued to thrive in that neighborhood.

I was deeply disappointed by the lack of engagement from the faith community and especially from those whose congregations were in some of the areas with the most gang activity. Unfortunately, I was beginning to develop a better understanding of institutions and their propensity to care mostly about their own welfare more than anything else. I expected more than this type of self-centeredness from the religious leaders we invited to city hall, but at the end of the summer, they had spent most of the time lamenting all that was wrong and being concerned about getting grant funds. They did not put their faith into action for the sake of the community. Instead, they were more interested in perpetuating their own programs and funding. Thus, the work that we began when I was there ended when the current mayor's term ended.

During this time, I met General Colin Powell, whom I had a chance to speak with at the United States Conference of Mayors' annual meeting, a few months before it was time for me to leave the mayor's office. He was a public official who impressed me. I liked General Powell because he seemed consistent and courageous. He was also the chair of the Points of Light Foundation, which supported the Corporation for National and Community Service (best known as AmeriCorps).

When I was working at the mayor's office, I was able to bring my sons into the work. This was an important learning experience for them, and frankly, it was helpful for me as well, since I was raising them on my own and often didn't have childcare. My youngest son, who was eleven at the time, had a chance to participate in a panel discussion about video game violence with Senator Max Cleland. This was because we hosted a town hall for him. Though I was not teaching, I was still managing the administrative portion of the African American studies program and overseeing the work at Aunt Maggie's Kitchen Table, a family resource center located in Anthony Homes, a public housing complex. It was far too much work for me to be managing. I was raising two boys on my own and still dealing with rheumatoid arthritis. I am not actually sure how I did all that I did. However, a big part of my ability to manage came from my sons' willingness to be a part of my work and to accompany me on the journey. We ate too many fast-food dinners while traveling from one event to another. Homework was done in the back of rooms where I was leading meetings. My youngest son was often his own babysitter. I would pay him for each hour that he could manage himself while he was with me and I was working. This gave me a chance to do my work without his interruptions unless he really needed me. I'm not sure what this might have taught him, but he did manage to do this quite effectively, and he seemed glad to tally up his earnings whenever the workshops or meetings came to a close.

Along with my successes, I had a few failures. One of the most unfortunate ones involved contracting with a colleague at Mercer to make a video of my work with young people. I thought he had technical skills, which might have been the case, but it was not evident by the product he produced. He brought his camera equipment to our gatherings and took photos, and I had assumed he was recording as well. I had no skills in this area, so I was not really able to assess what he was doing. He came to several events and spent a fair amount of time on the project. Finally, he told me the video was finished. I should have sat with him to preview it, but I did not.

I invited my city hall colleagues to come screen the video with me a few days later. When we put the video in the machine, it had not one bit of sound. All he had given me for the five hundred dollars I paid him was a silent slideshow of photographs. I was more embarrassed than angry. I was sorry I had not watched the video before I invited others to screen it with me. I will never make that mistake again as long as I live. When I tried to talk to the videographer about the problems with the video, he gave me a good dose of double talk, and the conversation went absolutely nowhere.

Some months following this disastrous mess, I was able to contract with a person who made an actual video, titled *Turning Weapons into Plowshares*. We at the mayor's office were able to use this video quite well to talk about our mural painting and gun buybacks when giving presentations on youth violence prevention to parents and others. Some people in Macon criticized my efforts to keep this work in front of the media. The critique of my being overly concerned about media support was not well founded. However, there are times when it takes far too much energy to try to set the story straight. I was willing to live with the criticism. I knew what I was attempting. Violence was an urgent issue during this era. I thought we needed to get all the support and help we could get from every corner of the community. Our children's lives were at stake. That seemed like a good enough reason to be as assertive as possible in finding all the possible resources, including resources in the media.

CHAPTER 8

There were personal failings that came within this two-year period too. I forgot speaking engagements on two occasions. I was mortified about that. One time I traveled to Maryland to lead workshops on violence prevention. I was expected to be in one small town the first day and another small town the second. I had to drive directly from the airport to the town where the workshop was to take place. I went to the wrong city, having mixed it up with the city I was supposed to visit the following day. I had to drive back to the correct place, where I gave the worst workshop I have ever given because I was too tired and ill prepared. It was such a long and painful day. The next day was a little better but not much. I was glad to get back home. I was attempting to make financial ends meet by leading workshops along with everything else I was doing. However, these efforts were clearly not working well. I learned an important lesson on that Maryland trip. While it was very difficult to pay attention to what was happening, I had to.

I became aware that I had to shift my rhythm. I was one person, and I was managing arthritis, my sons, and working in the mayor's office, as well as continuing to manage the family resource center located in a public housing facility where all the children were on free and reduced lunches. I had far too much work to do, and the work I was doing was incredibly stressful. Thinking and speaking about violence every day became exhausting. I realized that my sons needed me to stay well so that I would be able to take care of them. The way I was going, my wellness was not being supported. I knew something had to change.

A few weeks before I finished my work at the mayor's office, the dean of Wesleyan College, a predominantly white women's college, along with a faculty member, came to speak to me about coming to Wesleyan to receive the Clara Carter Acree Distinguished Professor of Socio-Cultural Studies Chair, an endowed chair honoring a Wesleyan alumna.

134

It was almost time for me to return to Mercer. At Mercer, I would be doing basically what I was doing before I had left to be the loaned executive. In the meantime, a new professor had been hired in the English department who was working to undermine me as the director of the African American studies program because he wanted the position, though he never even hinted as much. In my effort to be transparent, I had told him that African American studies was not my primary discipline. This was true, though I had an interdisciplinary PhD that combined this subject area and Jungian psychology. Well, he wasted no time going to the dean to see if he could get me removed and have the program placed under his direction. I was dumbfounded by his behavior.

I had so many lessons to learn. But the situation that developed around the African American studies program with this new professor who was not satisfied to simply be an English teacher taught me about being more careful when speaking. My commitment to transparency had caused me to create suffering for myself at previous times in my life. It was important for me to learn that my integrity was not dependent on my saying all the truth I could think of every time I opened my mouth. I was being shown that there are times when you simply do not need to speak. While I didn't allow folks such as these to make me become a person I don't wish to be, I paid attention to the lessons they taught me, and I am much better than I used to be at discerning when to speak and what to say to whom. I learned to remain silent unless speaking improves the silence. It is not the silence of voicelessness but the empowered voice choosing silence that brings forth new energy and life. It is a terrible tragedy not to be able to speak, but it is a joyous moment to realize you can speak and to choose silence instead because silence is the better choice. It is empowering to become aware of this and to practice it.

The amazing thing is that, just when this English professor was trying to push me out, I received the invitation to
relocate to Wesleyan. Wesleyan was also in Macon and was
actually closer to my house than Mercer. For a few minutes
I hated to think of telling Mercer's president, who had been
so generous, that I was not coming back. However, all my
concern was erased when I witnessed how glad he was for
me. He seemed to have no problem at all with the fact that I
was not coming back.

I knew immediately that the invitation to Wesleyan was
something I should say yes to. I was able to avoid a battle
with the person eager to take over African American studies. Rather than having to figure out how to work with him,
I simply offered my resignation and went to clean out my
office. I went directly from my position as a loaned executive
in the mayor's office to my new job as an endowed chair at
Wesleyan, for a healthy pay increase and far less stress and
work. Many lessons and chances to see the world through a
new lens came during this time. At times, I wondered how
to navigate the many threads of my life that seemed to keep
presenting themselves without much of an invitation from
me. I was not always sure what to do with them, but I knew
I could not ignore them. All the things that kept falling into
place reinforced my understanding that the way to live my
life was to stay intentional and to trust that there was a loving parent in the universe looking after my sons and me.

I was jubilant about my new job. I didn't have to move in
order to have this new experience. I would not be forced to be
in a new city and face all the challenges that come with such a
relocation. Yet I had the benefit of embracing a new community. I was very curious about what it would be like to work
with female students only. While I love my sons and have
great respect and regard for many men, I thrive on teaching,
coaching, and encouraging women. Thus, the opportunity

to be in this institution held a lot of promise for me to grow in new ways and to use my gifts in new ways as well. I completed my first year at Wesleyan very successfully. My classes went well. I got involved in some of the redevelopment work that was being done. I was glad to be there and to work with the women students. We did a lot of work around the issue of HIV/AIDS. We also talked incessantly about women's issues and the things we could be doing as a college focusing on women. The conversations were uplifting.

I had no way to know that this institution was far from being what I was imagining it to be. For one thing, the then-current president, installed in 1997, was the first woman to be appointed to that post. For a women's college, this was a startling inconsistency. The president was far from what many people felt was the right person for the college. I didn't know what was going on. I went to faculty meetings. I was busy trying to get acclimated to being there and learning where things were on the campus. The more I learned, the more I saw that many things were not working. I met the president and she seemed personable, but it is not easy to learn much from a short conversation with a person who is trying to make a good impression on you. So my conversations with her were not very revealing.

The dissatisfaction with the president grew considerably worse by the end of my second year. In the beginning of my third year, the handwriting was on the wall. I will never forget the faculty meeting with the college trustees, in which we were to talk about what was wrong with the way things were going. My colleagues were failing to say the truth about the toxic manner in which the president governed, something we all agreed on and talked about all the time. I couldn't stand it, so I finally stood up and said what no one else would say. I named all the ways the environment was toxic and not the place I thought it was when I first came to work here, and I described how saddened I was that we had an environment that was causing so much trouble for everyone. After I spoke, a few others chimed in. I was dumbfounded by the level of fear these adults seemed to have in regard to the administration and, I suppose, the trustees. I'm not sure what that was about, but telling the truth was needed that day. Twenty-four hours later, the president offered her resignation. My colleagues kept complimenting me for speaking up. I lost respect for many of them because some of them did not speak up that day, and the ones who did were not willing to do so until I had spoken. I was cordial to my colleagues and said thank you to their words of affirmation, but I noted not to trust them or to count on them in any manner as long as I was in that environment. I was so glad to witness myself as a person who was not voiceless, unlike my many colleagues who had allowed themselves to be made voiceless. After I discovered that I had a voice, I never thought there was a job that was worth making me voiceless out of fear of losing the job. I think I believed that having a voice and being willing to use it would be enough to get me through life, as long as I was willing to be courageous and to tell the truth.

The first woman to be selected as president left after five years and was replaced by a former graduate. We were all delighted. A committee was appointed to work on healing the wounds that had been inflicted over the past five years by having a president who was the author of massive workplace toxicity. I was selected to cochair that committee, with someone whom I respected and had enjoyed working with in the past. In many ways, it all seemed somewhat surreal to me, because I was not expecting to be called upon to stand up so much as a courageous voice on the campus. However, I was comforted by the reminder that I was really in earth school, and everything was about learning. We headed down the road of seeking to see how the college could become better at service, though that did not turn out to be what most folks really wanted. For the most part, I'm not sure if many folks knew exactly what they wanted. I think we got caught up in trying to fix a lot of extraneous issues, and it impacted the work of our committee in negative ways, deterring us from our core objective.

I had made a fairly good reputation for myself by now at Wesleyan because I had imagined, designed, and found the funding to start the Lane Center for Community Service. Later, I helped secure the million-dollar endowment for it from two former students who were wealthy and interested in service. The last name of one of the donors was Lane, so the facility was named for her, though she was not especially interested in that happening. The center sponsored many programs related to service. It also sponsored a workday that the entire school participated in because classes were canceled, allowing us all to go into the community to do pre-arranged work projects for the day.

During this time, I staged a one-woman protest about the way one of my colleagues had been unfairly terminated over immigration issues related to her visa status, which the college had helped to create by not getting some of her documents filed properly. I did not show up for a campus-wide convocation in protest of what had happened to her. This was the same day I was to be presented with an award for excellent teaching. However, due to my protest, I was not there to receive it. Everybody was supposed to be there because faculty never missed convocations. But neither the president nor the dean had the courage to ask me why I wasn't there or to say anything to me about not being there. They already knew why I wasn't there, as I had gone on record in support of the former college employee who had been treated in such an inhumane manner. I was fascinated by the administration's lack of questions regarding the matter.

One particularly transformative project I was involved in during my time at Wesleyan was Aunt Maggie's Kitchen Table. Aunt Maggie's was not my idea. I was engaged in many conversations with the person who imagined it in the first place. At first, we believed we had the same vision. But when we got to the point of creating a viable working organization, all the conflicting ideas between me and the person whose idea it was in the beginning became irreconcilable. She wanted to create a respite center for single mothers, and I wanted to create more of a family services center with an afterschool program and a Saturday school for children who needed extra academic help. She chose to vacate the project. Perhaps it would have been a great idea for me to do the same and simply let it die. But my will to make things work was too powerful, and I jumped in with both feet and began to do what I knew how to do.

Aunt Maggie's Kitchen Table became a family resource center. It was located in a public housing facility. We were fortunate enough to have two three-bedroom apartments made available to us by the Macon Housing Authority for a rental fee of just two dollars a year. I was never paid for the work I did at Aunt Maggie's, although it was the place where I worked the hardest since I left the sharecropping fields of my father, where I was picking cotton in Arkansas during late summers with temperatures in the nineties. I used students to do the majority of the work at Aunt Maggie's, but I had to do all the coordinating and envisioning. We had a few opportunities to pay for reception assistance, and we had a little office support from AmeriCorps and its Foster Grandparents program. But most of the work was done by volunteers, and most of them were my students. It became a service arm for Wesleyan when I was there.

We taught computer classes, etiquette classes, and photography classes. We held Saturday school. We had a decent library for younger children and many books that children could take home as they wished. We helped the children who came to the afterschool program obtain library cards and build bookshelves so that they could have a small library at home. We had some of the Saturday school children write their own stories, which we published as books. One copy of the book was theirs to keep, and one went to their school library. We tutored children and mentored them as best we could. We partnered with MidSummer Macon to provide the children in the housing complex a summer arts enrichment program, which they would not have even heard about if we had not been in their community. We helped bury people who died without money to pay for a funeral. We helped people fill prescriptions when they couldn't afford the medicine otherwise. We acquired house furnishings and other basic necessities for families who needed them.

So much of what we were able to do was the result of my making connections with folks in the community who were willing to assist us. For instance, once a mother died, leaving six children to fend for themselves. We discovered that they didn't have beds, blankets, towels, and other basics. One of our friends who owned a linen store gave the children everything they needed and found other vendors to give them mattresses and things she didn't carry. She was generous in the same way when I led Wesleyan College in building a woman a Habitat for Humanity house. She provided all the linens and curtains and, again, found others to provide what her store didn't carry. These relationships were crucial to our survival because we got only one grant from the Knight Foundation, a gift from a local businessman, and small donations from various donors to help us.

Wesleyan College applied for the Jimmy and Rosalynn Carter Award the first year that it was given for outstanding campus-community collaboration. They cited Aunt

Maggie's as their community partnership. We won and were given five thousand dollars and a couple of new computers. I had thought that the publicity would have helped open more doors for us than it actually did. After we won, we received a visit from Mrs. Rosalynn Carter, and that was an amazing day for us. But even her visit didn't do much to improve our lot in terms of funding—although perhaps it did help us to recruit a few famous guests. For example, we brought the nationally known poet Nikki Giovanni to Aunt Maggie's the day she was speaking at Wesleyan, and people from the community brought their poetry. We sat outside in a big circle, and they read their poems to Giovanni. She told me that was the very best part of her visit with us. It was an amazing day for all the folks in our little community. Poor folks who live in public housing are not used to having nationally known poets and a former First Lady pay visits to their neighborhoods.

We did meals on Thursdays and invited our senior citizens who were living in the complex to lunch, many of whom were living in isolation. Some of them wouldn't see anyone for the week except us and the folks who were at Aunt Maggie's for lunch. The meals got out of hand for a bit with folks who had less need showing up because it was a nice lunch of soup and cornbread and at times a salad or simple dessert. We finally got a handle on it. The disingenuous folks looking for a free lunch got tired of us. I think our simple soup and bread menu was not adequate for them. They stopped coming, and it was a good day for us when that happened.

Recently I encountered a young professional woman who is running a foundation for one of the gentlemen who generously supported Aunt Maggie's along the way. She told me she had lived in the complex during the time that Aunt Maggie's was thriving and that because of us, she attended Mid-Summer Macon's art program, which brought students from around the city to live at Wesleyan College for six weeks and engage in art, music, drama, and dance. Our children from the public housing facility were commuters, so we had them bused to the campus each day.

So the circle just enlarges as time goes on. Many people had their lives positively impacted because we were present. There were days when we needed to do big tasks for folks in our sphere, but many days we just needed to provide a newspaper to a child so he could complete an assignment that would not have been done if we had not been there because there would not have been an available newspaper and the family didn't have money to purchase one.

It is impossible to know the good or the harm you have done at times. I cannot begin to assess our work at Aunt Maggie's other than in inadequate, quantifiable ways having to do with how many children we served, the number of children who went on a field trip, and things like that. But qualitatively, which is more about transformation, we simply have to trust that we had an impact. I'm glad we did it. Aunt Maggie's turned out to be a good resource in a community of great desolation. We know our presence mattered.

My voice of advocacy was stronger now than ever before. I had many opportunities to be in the public school that all the children in our housing complex attended. The entire school was on free lunch. The housing complex and the school are in an impoverished community that used to be far more viable than it was then or is today. But I always made it clear to those who wished to volunteer with us that the only difference between the folks in this community and the ones in their own communities was the lack of economic resources. Every person who lived in that community was a beloved child of the Creator, and anyone who wished to volunteer with us had to be clear about that fact. The principal at the school did not share my perspective.

I knew I would have to report the disrespectful behaviors she exhibited toward students and their parents as well as her staff at times. She was verbally abusive. I was not happy to see her or anyone else get into trouble, but she was making life worse for children whose lives were already challenging. The principal's behavior indicated that she had no respect for the folks in her building, whether they were coworkers, parents, or children. I had lived a lot around that type of denigrating energy, and I knew how much injury it causes. I could not stand by and say nothing. Reluctantly, I reported the principal to the superintendent, and she was dealt with.

"My lips shall speak for miseries that have no mouth," writes the Martinican poet Aimé Césaire. This line has stayed with me since the day I first read it. Of course, it is very important to be careful in making such an assessment in the first place. If someone has no voice, they have been rendered rather helpless. It is important to be careful about naming a person as helpless. But when it is clear that voicelessness is an issue, there is an opportunity to see what can be done on behalf of the voiceless one. However, I have come to understand that in speaking for the voiceless in whatever way that might occur, it is critical to try to demonstrate to them that they can speak indeed, even if they cannot speak about whatever issue is at hand.

The speaking can then embody a different energy that becomes the source of assistance to the voiceless and perhaps can help them discover what they can speak about. One of Aunt Maggie's clients/supporters, a resident in the housing complex, told me one day that she knew we cared about the folks who lived there because we went to their funerals. Whenever someone passed on whom we had worked with in any manner, we took the time to attend their funeral. I didn't think much about it because it is simply what you do when you care to be respectful. The resident's observation spoke volumes to me about how there are many ways to speak. Behavior can carry on a loud and robust conversation in any community. It is often impossible to hear what a person is saying because their behavior stands in absolute contradiction to their proclamation.

The strengthening of my voice of advocacy was partially the result of my gaining more clarity about the things I believed to be worth being an advocate for. However, as I look back, it is clear that my call to become a prophetic witness was emerging as well. At an earlier point in my journey, I would not have known that I could stand with my colleague at Wesleyan who was banned from her office and treated like a criminal because of a paperwork issue regarding her immigration status that the college should have helped her resolve before it got to the point of no return. It never crossed my mind to worry about what would happen to me if I stood in solidarity with her. All the faculty should have stood with her, but there was too much fear floating around for any of them to do that, even though they knew she was not being treated in a fair and decent manner.

Standing with her by simply reaching out to her was a good act, but it was clear to me that my witness needed to be more public. Standing with someone in a private manner is quite different from choosing to make a public statement. My public statement was my one-person boycott of the convocation that faculty were not allowed to miss unless there was an extreme emergency. And the angels and heavenly host were affirming my public witness because it was the day I was given a teaching award, and I was not there to accept it. Thus my public witness became even louder.

The energy and courage to publicly bear witness to my understanding of the truth had arrived in me and I had not realized it. It was a long time after that incident with my Wesleyan colleague before I was willing to think of myself as having a voice as a prophetic witness. Of course, it made sense because I had begun to name many of the ills in the institutions I had to engage with. I named these ills for what they were, and for the most part, I was not concerned about the consequences that might come to me.

Over the course of many years, I have taken the steps that seemed to make sense for the life that was unfolding in front of me. In the situation with my colleague, I had been led to the place of bearing witness, and not just for that one time, but as an ongoing practice. From now on, I would have to live out of that space in the best ways I could, regardless of the consequences. From this new vantage point, I looked on in wonder at the journey before me.

9

New Frontiers

IN 2012, A FRIEND ASKED IF I would come to Atlanta and spend the day meeting with her about a book she was writing. I happily agreed. We met at Whole Foods and got ourselves comfortably nestled into a booth, where she spread out her notes. We had a day of good conversation, good food, and good vibrations from being in that space. I enjoy watching people, and there were so many who looked like folks I would have enjoyed speaking with if I had the chance. Many appeared to be from other parts of the world, and I enjoy talking to people who were not born in the US. It was a memorable day.

As I drove home that day, I reflected on how much I had enjoyed being in Atlanta. I always felt good energy in that city. Whenever I traveled outside Macon and returned, I could tell when I got to the city limits, even if there were no signs. There was a shift in my energy, and I knew I was back in Bibb County. While it is a little difficult to explain, there was a sense of freedom outside Macon for me that seemed to disappear whenever I returned to the city. My soul was more connected to that energetic vibration than I realized. But af-

ter spending the day in Atlanta and experiencing the goodness of the day, I knew it was time to relocate to Atlanta.

I had been in Macon for forty years. Though I came to
Georgia to live and work in Atlanta, all my employment had
been in Macon, with the exception of the one year I lived in
Memphis, Tennessee. I had left Los Angeles for Georgia in
search of that "New South" described by Julian Bond in his
biography as a place that was more accepting of all people
and that had become more interested in justice than injustice.
Unfortunately, the South was not as new as I had imagined
while I was still living in the comfort of California, reading
Julian Bond's *Black Rebel* as if it were a romance novel. Of
course, the South was new in many ways. Much of the old-
guard segregation was gone. There were many African Americans, including Bond, emerging as leaders. But Atlanta was
quite a bit different in spirit than the rest of Georgia. Macon
was holding on to as many of its old ways as possible. I caught
a glimpse of what Macon was going to be like when I went
there for the first time in 1972. As I entered the city limits,
there were billboards espousing a policy to shoot robbers to
kill them. These billboards were purchased by a former mayor
who was called Machine Gun Ronnie and had a reputation for
being horrible. He also had obtained a tank from somewhere
that was to become a part of the police equipment. Who was
this tank intended to be used against, and why were they considered the enemy, to be attacked with military force? I had
thought I had walked backward into the past because I was so
blindsided by the racism that met me when I tried to rent an
apartment in one of those renovated antebellum houses, but
not a single owner would rent to me.

After four-plus decades, I was delighted to know I was
finally going to leave this place that I had never intended as
a permanent place of residence. I decided on that day, being
in Atlanta with my friend, that it was time to leave Macon.

A year later, after I retired from Wesleyan, I moved into a lovely two-bedroom apartment in Clayton County, which put me about an hour from Macon and twenty-five minutes from downtown Atlanta. This was perfect for me because I could get back to Macon to visit my friends but have the advantage of being in downtown Atlanta whenever I wanted. There were days when I could see a school of deer in the parking lot where I lived because we had woods close by. I enjoyed birds, squirrels, rabbits, and deer on a regular basis from my balcony. It was delightful.

Before making the decision to retire, a number of incidents led me to discern that my path was leading away from academia. I realized I was ready after thirty-four years to have a respite from the people in higher education who were draining my energy. I wrote a letter of resignation effective at the end of the 2007/8 school year. I was sixty-two years old. There were administrators who were quite unhappy with my decision. After all, I was the bright, shiny remedy to their lack of racial and ethnic diversity at Wesleyan. The college was over a hundred years old and still had only two faculty members of color. Along with this, it had some strong historical connections to the Ku Klux Klan that it was not proud about. A part of the reason I was hired as an endowed chair was related to my high level of community visibility. I had been at Wesleyan nine years, and I was leaving. For some unknown reason, they were unwilling to allow me to receive emerita status, which is an honor for retiring academics. It was probably the same reason they had not given me tenure when they hired me, though I didn't really concern myself about the tenure piece because I decided that an endowed chair–holding professor was not going to be fired unless I did something illegal or immoral. I was a bit disappointed not to receive emerita status because it indicates that one has retired and served well. But I recovered rather quickly because I remembered that institutions are not to be counted on to care about anything except what supports their agenda. I believe that I was tampering with their image and agenda, and I had to be punished in some manner. Along with this, my going-away party was not nearly as nice as the parties that had been thrown for other retiring faculty. But if the president is unhappy with you, then you need to be prepared to suffer the consequences, and I had stood up against the institution in ways that the administration preferred I had not. But my commitment to truth telling and my personal integrity were more important to me than their titles, parties, or opinion of me. I believe their not giving me emerita status and giving me a a rather mediocre retirement party were about the most pain-causing things they could do to me as they sought to register their displeasure with me in their usual passive-aggressive ways. It made me even happier to be getting away from the energy-draining behaviors that were so alive and well in that space.

There are many examples of unfortunate behavior in these academic spaces. However, a couple of examples should illustrate the overall institutional attitude that caused me to be concerned and to grieve. As you will recall, I spearheaded the wonderful project of honoring one hundred African American women in Macon and Middle Georgia over a nine-year period. The final portions of the project and official launching of the book featuring all the women were done at Wesleyan. I will never forget sitting on the stage with the president of Wesleyan and having her turn to me and comment that the book was so much better than she thought it was going to be. I didn't know how to respond, so I said nothing. What a denigrating and disrespectful comment to make to a scholar-activist who was an endowed chair holder. It spoke volumes about her attitude toward me and African American culture, and it was not a comment I felt like bothering to engage. The coffee-table book, *Standing on Their Shoulders: The Celebration of the Wisdom of African American Women*, was beautiful and well done. Each woman had two pages in the book: one for her photograph, and the page beside it for her biographical information. It was published by the Tubman African American Museum through a grant given to them for such projects.

Along with the book, we had placed in the main auditorium the lovely, very large portrait of all one hundred women standing together on the steps of the Macon City Auditorium, which the photographer had donated to Wesleyan. It was striking. But I am sure that many of the those who did not wish to see Black photographs so prominently displayed who visited the campus for events in that auditorium were not as excited about it as I was because the photograph of all of those beautiful Black women was certainly conflicting with their idea of the predominantly white campus environment they cherished and sought to maintain.

After I retired, the portrait was taken down and placed, without any attempt to preserve it, in a closet in the art department basement. At some point someone found it and decided it should be given to the African American woman who worked in the Student Life Office to see what she might do with it. How interesting that an African American was charged with finding a suitable place for the portrait and given additional labor as well. She placed it in the Lane Center, which I had designed and founded while I was a professor. She was kind enough to call and let me know what had happened and the process she had to go through to seek a suitable place for it. Eventually it was moved to the student center, displayed alongside a short explanation of its significance.

When I heard what had happened to the portrait, I called to speak to the dean, a person of faith who was known for caring about integrity and racial justice. She proved to not care about either one of them when it came to this issue. In our conversation, she told me not to worry about it. After all, she reminded me, I must have forgotten that I was not there any longer. This made me so angry. I had allowed myself to believe there was some genuine care and concern for the issues of race and equity at Wesleyan, since they talked about it and had hired me. I had spent my life caring about and seeking to find and lead others onto a healing path, and I had expected that institution to do the same. But it was the same old story that racist systems always employ. Do as little as possible and nothing that is too costly. Then try to look as good as possible in the progressive arena while making sure that not too much has to change in your environment. Hold on to your power, control, and white supremacy. Yes, it was the same old story. I had forgotten for a moment where the truth really resides.

The other incident was quite different but equally as instructive. Macon enjoyed the presence of Dr. Harold Katner, an amazing infectious disease physician who had risked his well-being during the height of the HIV/AIDS crisis and who had given more than twenty years of his life to treating patients when resources were scarce. For decades, he had worked to find support services for his patients so that they could work toward recovery or die with dignity. He is an amazingly compassionate person, a phenomenal role model for selfless servant leadership. He went about this work quietly and was rarely commended for it. So when Jim Marshall, the former mayor for whom I had served as a loaned executive, was elected to the United States Congress, I decided it was an opportunity to seek a congressional commendation for the physician. Congressman Marshall's office was glad to assist us.

In 2003, I planned a lovely event for Dr. Katner, which brought all types of people to the Wesleyan campus. Many of them were patients and former patients. Our students participated in the program, and one of Congressman Marshall's staff came from Washington, DC, to present the commendation. We had a lovely reception, and there were so many tears of joy shed that day. Many people from the community at large voiced their deep gratitude to us at Wesleyan for doing this for him.

But while I was sitting on the stage with the president of Wesleyan—the second president during my time there—she turned to me and said she didn't know why on earth we were having this event. Again, I was dumbfounded. We were honoring one of Macon's most loved and appreciated servant leaders, as we were a campus engaging in daily conversations about lifetime service, with an emphasis on servant-leadership development. I did not respond to her comment. What was there to say? I don't really know what I could have said that would have made any difference whatsoever. I wondered what it would take to make the institution live up to its ideals when its own leaders didn't seem to understand the meaning of the words they constantly used to describe who they claimed they wanted to be.

After I left Wesleyan, I had no idea what it would be like to do what I was about to do. I began by getting all my work done and my office cleaned out by graduation. I was happy to surrender my keys and fascinated to see how promptly they removed me from email access and lists. They were clearly in a rush to begin the process of forgetting I had been there. One of the many mistaken assumptions they must have made was that I was interested in being their designated Negro, who would be willing to put my head down and quietly go along with whatever was done, and that my joy about that role would lead me to abdicate the call to be a prophetic voice in that place. They were wrong, and they seemed to have chosen a new path that will prevent them from making that mistake again as they dismantled the program that I led and moved the endowed chair that I held into the business department. The chair was intended to be focused on socio-cultural and social-justice matters, which would provide a person who embraced justice and equality issues.

It was liberating to think that I could reimagine my work and way of being in the world. As I'd done many times before in my life, I opened myself to a discernment process. I was ready to say yes to a new season of life. I decided I was going to become an herbalist and a craftswoman. I had learned so much about the healing properties of herbs and oils when I sought many of them as remedies to help manage my arthritis. My mother was really a folk medicine sort of woman who could imagine ways to address most ailments. She would have been better at it if there had been fewer survival challenges before her. She knew so much, which was mostly passed on to her from our elders. She paid close attention to those who came before her. There was hardly any ailment we could name for which Mama could not find a remedy. There were times when I thought she would cause us to die with some of those remedies because they did not taste good. But I must quickly confess that I thought the same thing when she cooked things like squash or spinach. Of course, I was wrong, and now I wish I had paid better attention to some of the remedies she used. I had my mother as a model for how to live as an herbalist. As I was looking to my future, I was also looking to my past. I decided that making aroma-therapy products, candles, and greeting cards would become my work after retiring from being a professor and activist. Seeking to get on this path had something to do with my on-going quest to be liberated. I needed to know that I could use my hands as well as my brain to make things. I needed to reconnect to the essentials in my psyche in some deeper way, and entering onto this path for a bit was almost as transformative as going to West Africa had been, what seemed like a lifetime before.

The first three months of being retired from the academic world did not seem real. I kept waking up in the middle of the night in a panic about not getting ready for the beginning of school. It finally settled into my psyche that I had no classes. I finally moved on inside my head and heart from the concern about not being ready for the school year that I was not going to have.

I really like jewelry, especially vintage jewelry, and one of my friends invited me to volunteer in her jewelry store. She gave me a lot of jewelry that she had decided to discard or that was left over after sales. She had so much that it was easy for her to do, and it made me a very happy person. I learned a lot about the mechanics of making good jewelry. I also learned who many of the best jewelry makers were, and what to pay attention to when assessing the quality of pieces of jewelry. It was wonderful. I went once a week to help my friend, and it was such a delight. The routine was good for me, and it was helpful to get into a world that I knew so little about, to experience the energy systems in an arena that was such a contrast to the academic world I had lived in for such a long time. The jewelry world was far more about experience than about having to read and analyze student work and seeking ways to engage students in the process of learning while seeking a path to growth that did not always seem viable to them and caused that work to be challenging. I really enjoyed working with my friend at her jewelry store because it was pleasant to do the work that was required with a fair amount of detachment.

The connection with my jeweler friend led me more deeply into the art world. I attended events that I wouldn't have known about or chosen to attend without the urging of my friend. During this time, I also made greeting cards. My friend sold them in her store. I was so happy and affirmed by that fact. I love art, though I cannot draw or paint. My greeting cards became little pieces of art.

Butterflies are a very powerful symbolic energy force for me because they represent transformation. I take great delight in seeing them, working with them in card design, and even wearing them as pieces of jewelry. I made cards using butterflies made of paper, which I found in various art stores, and handmade paper. The cards turned out very nicely, and people really liked them. I sold many of them. One of my friends bought hundreds of dollars' worth—literally five hundred dollars at one time—of my cards. They were five dollars each, and he commissioned me to make one hundred for him. I was so honored to be asked.

At the time, my sons were living away in their own places. I still had our two dogs—which were good company for me, though difficult to manage at times—but I turned the house into a craft shop. I bought metal shelves and filled them with supplies. Materials for candle making and card making, all kinds of essential oils, containers of every imaginable size, glue sticks for my hot glue gun, beautiful handmade paper, and all the other supplies I needed filled up the living room, dining room, hallway, and kitchen. The handmade paper source I found was phenomenal. There must have been thousands of designs and types of paper at that website, and it was not very expensive. I would sit for hours looking at all the options and trying to decide what to buy. I didn't know that so much beauty could be found in paper. I would have made clothes for myself out of some of the paper if I could have.

I made body creams, candles, potpourri, and bath salts and oils, and headed to craft fairs and other venues where I could sell my products. I didn't realize how hard this work could be and how difficult it can be to sell anything. I needed to know much more than I did about the production and marketing of crafts. I worked hard because I always work hard at whatever I decide to do. I made products and took them to a lot of places. I sold many of them, but there were times when I would spend a day at a venue and sell little to none. So the idea I had about this becoming a second career began to seem further away than I had imagined when I first thought about it. It is like everything else: you can work hard, and you still may not do well.

I set up an online store. I had a friend make labels, which listed ingredients, for the products I made. As I write this today, I am smiling at my lack of knowledge about so many things and how comical I must have looked to those who did know about start-ups and the struggles you have to navigate and the hurdles that have to be overcome. Everyone, including folks at the chamber of commerce who helped folks like me, was supportive and gave me advice. I think the angels found this space a bit funny as well. They helped me, but I was in a bit over my head, and I didn't quite see my way forward.

Somewhere along the way I began to realize that it is not feasible to try to be a one-woman crafts business. It was too hard to make enough products to thrive. If I had someone place a large order of anything I was selling, I wouldn't have the capacity to produce it all. I had to interrogate myself about my long-term plans as I got into this more and more. Along with coming to terms with my limitations, I had to honestly assess how I was managing arthritis. Preparing my wares was far more taxing than preparing to teach classes or sitting in meetings before retirement. While the stress was different, there was some stress surrounding this effort. It was not financially viable at all. I was having fun, but I was not really making any money. I was very fortunate if I made back my investment in some of the products.

I've noticed a pattern in my life. When I begin to really focus on what I am doing and whether or not I should continue, there seems to be a shift in my energy and circumstances. In this case the shift came when I was challenged by a situation in the Episcopal diocese of Atlanta regarding the denomination's racial healing work. I had joined the Episcopal Church in 1980 and was invested in their progress.

In 2000, the General Convention of the Episcopal Church had passed a resolution requiring leaders in the Episcopal Church to participate in what they called antiracism training. Anyone who wished to be ordained as a priest or deacon was mandated to participate. The same was true for people who served on the vestry or on a search committee, or who worked in any leadership position. One of the biggest problems was the lack of a really good curriculum. But a curriculum was designed that helped provide a starting place. The larger problem was that the adopted resolution was not clear about what would happen if people chose not to engage in this work. Thus, it was not evenly implemented across the entire denomination.

In the diocese of Atlanta, people hated the day-long training and would do whatever they could to avoid it. It wasn't that hard to avoid because some rectors did not enforce compliance. But there were two people who stepped up to the plate to lead the training in our diocese. They wanted to have two days for it, but the bishop didn't see the wisdom in making it two days when people hated it so much.

Before I moved to Atlanta, I had complained to the bishop that I didn't think the work on racism was good enough. I said he needed to do something about it. Much to my dismay, he put me on the Anti-Racism Commission. I was not trying to get any more work to do, but if you complain about something not being done to your liking, you have to be willing to be a part of the solution. I was an African American studies professor, and I taught many courses on prejudice and racism, so I had more than a passing interest in the way the work was being done. Because I had been confirmed in the Episcopal Church many years before, I had kept an eye on the quality of the racial healing work that was being done, and I knew that it could be improved.

A few months after I moved to Atlanta, the commission was informed that there had not been any classes offered for a while because the two persons who had been leading the work had resigned without having any replacements. Many folks were waiting to be ordained but still needed to do the antiracism training. The diocese had to provide access to the mandated classes.

When I heard about this dilemma, I thought to myself, *I hope they work it out.* I was retired from that hard work of trying to help folks navigate their way through race. I wanted to keep enjoying my respite from it. But the chair of the commission kept talking about it at each meeting, and finally it became clear that I needed to offer to lead the workshop. After all, there was not any reason for me not to. I told the chair I would take on the work, and I called the bishop's office to let them know and to see if they could recommend someone to assist me.

The bishop's office made a recommendation, and I made contact with the person. We agreed that we would be able to work together. We set about to carve a day's workshop out of material that was originally intended to be a two-day workshop. I decided that since we were working with folks in the Episcopal Church, we should include the Eucharist. So we added the Eucharist to our workshop day, and I called the training "Eucharist-Centered Training." It was primarily that modification that changed the response we got from participants in the workshops we presented.

The previous model was centered on diversity training, but my coleader and I reimagined the day as a part of the spiritual formation of the participants. Adding the Eucharist helped make explicit that the day was about more than diversity training. We worked hard to change the focus from a one-day event that had to be tolerated before the completion box could be checked, to the start of an ongoing and transformative labor. One day's work was not enough to eradicate racism from people's lives. We argued that racism is a chronic illness that has to be managed on a daily basis for as long as one is alive and that this is a part of one's spiritual formation. Most people of faith understand the idea of lifetime growth and development as part of the responsibility you commit to when you connect to whatever faith community you choose. Addressing racism, we argued, is an area for growth. Within a few months, we had changed the face of the training. Instead of being a chore, it was something people were beginning to seek out. Parishes started inviting us to come and present to groups in their parishes. We were delighted to do that in the early days because we needed to establish a constituency of support and affirmation. We needed to know that there was growing commitment to this work. The more commitment there was, the more we would attract the attention of people we hadn't yet reached.

The classes filled up quickly. Most folks felt that they were quite beneficial. A few times we had very reluctant participants who tried to disrupt the day. Once or twice, we met outright hostility, which the person managed to hold on to for the entire length of the workshop. It was always sad to see such resistance because the resister was the greatest loser and probably would never realize it. As the word spread throughout our diocese, our wider church family began to inquire about our classes and wondered if they could send people to participate in them. We had several small groups come to participate from around the country. Before, people were doing everything they could to avoid the workshop. Now, we needed to offer ten to twelve workshops a year.

In 2012, the Anti-Racism Commission chair stepped down and asked if I would be interested in chairing the group. I was delighted. I knew that so much work needed to be done, and I knew how to do it. When I became chair, one of our first acts was to rename the commission. The bishop of the diocese, who had been newly elected that year, had encouraged us to do so, and I was very much in favor of it because new energy was needed and a new name seemed fitting. A few people in the group were not sure about pushing for the change. Three or four of the members chose to retire from the group. They had served a long time and they were fatigued, so retiring was a good idea.

We changed the name from the "Anti-Racism Commission" to "Beloved Community: Commission for Dismantling Racism." We talked about how the name embodied our mission. We had to help make space for the beloved community, the place where all God's children can be free to be born. In order to do that, we had to dismantle racism. After changing the name, we added several new members. Previously, all our meetings had been held in one of the large downtown parishes. Now we took our monthly meetings on the road and invited parishes to host. We alternated between mornings and afternoons, inviting the hosting parish to join us and to provide breakfast or lunch, whichever one was needed. These changes helped to make the commission the people's commission, and people began to see the work as belonging to them.

The commission organized diocese-wide book studies, film screenings, pilgrimages, conversations on race, and other activities to support the one-day workshops. Our reputation grew tremendously. Bishops brought groups to Atlanta to learn from us. We were invited to be one of the two dioceses that presented to representatives from the House of Bishops and the House of Deputies when they were discussing ways to move the work of racial healing beyond a simple one-day workshop requirement. I am always a little mystified at how difficult it seems to be for folks to see how to do some of the things that are simple but touted as being impossible or nearly impossible.

We were already doing what they were trying to find a way to articulate. We had demonstrated in the diocese of Atlanta that the task of doing this work better was not as difficult as folks made it seem. I think we talk too much about many things that we need to get busy working on. However, I realize that a lot of the talking is a way to avoid the hard work and often disrupting decisions that have to be made if there is to be any sustainable systemic change. It's not enough to claim you want to solve a problem. All institutions are the same when it comes to this issue—so much talk, so little action—but it was disconcerting to see it in the faith community.

Our commitment to real change was good for our commission. We pursued the conversation with the presiding bishop because we were clearly already engaging in the work he was wishing to see. Our bishop agreed that we had outgrown being a commission. We were fifteen volunteers functioning as an organization, and I was working fifty or more hours a week managing all that our volunteer group was implementing. Yes, we had certainly outgrown ourselves. But I had been imagining that we would start a racial healing center of some type in Atlanta. I tried to have a conversation with a few folks about it, but they couldn't envision it, and that was the end of that conversation. I imagined that we could do the necessary work better as an organized center than a commission.

I was quite aggravated with myself that I was even bringing up the idea of a center because I had learned a long time ago that it is the rare person who can simply engage with you in a dream and be glad that you have it. What I had experienced was a lot of discouragement about a given idea unless it was something a person could discern their own role in. Oftentimes my visions did not include anyone in particular, so people resented them.

In spite of the lack of enthusiasm on the part of some on the commission, the bishop agreed we should approach the presiding bishop with the idea. We got marvelous support from several people on the presiding bishop's staff. He was pleased to see our proposal and agreed to join the diocese of Atlanta in a partnership to form a center. I was delighted and gathered a small group of folks to move us forward. We formed a board of advisors and began the challenging process of moving from being a commission to becoming a full-fledged center.

On October 7, 2017, we opened the Absalom Jones Episcopal Center for Racial Healing in the historic building that had housed only Episcopal Campus Ministry, which served the historic cluster of HBCUs across the street: Morris Brown College, Morehouse College, Spelman College, Clark Atlanta University, and the Interdenominational Theological Center. The old model of having a full-time priest as the campus minister had given way to part-time missioners by the time we opened the center. This allowed us to share space with the missioner.

When we were organizing the center, one young white person suggested we should have a priest, and he was more than likely thinking a white one, though that was not voiced. It is rare for white people to recommend Black and brown people for positions such as the director of new initiatives like this. I turned to the man who made the suggestion and clearly stated that the job was taken because I was going to run the center. After all, it had grown out of my vision and my desire to meet a need and a desire out in the world. These energies had come together to create this place, and I had been the one to channel these energies. It was ludicrous for someone to think I would do all this work and then walk off to let someone else implement it. That early conversation was grounded in many things, including ageism—after all, I was retired, and that meant I was old—and an incredulity that I as a Black woman would dare to see myself as the person who should assume this role.

The opening celebration of the center was a glorious day. It was attended by the presiding bishop, the bishop of Atlanta, and the bishop of Cape Coast, Ghana, our sister diocese in Africa. We had painted, washed, polished, and cleaned up the building so that everything was beautiful.

Later, we would remodel the front lobby so that visitors and students could have snacks, coffee, and a comfortable place to sit when visiting us. We transformed a building that was suffering from low energy and lack of interest to a place filled with warmth and welcome. Visitors tell us they can pick up the hospitable vibrations when entering our parking lot. We burn candles in our space. I am never in my home or office without a candle burning. It is a constant reminder of the day's prayers—of folks I want to remember throughout the day because they are having an especially hard time. It is also an affirmation that no light is too small to challenge the darkness. And besides all that, candles smell good and make the environment feel warmer and more welcoming.

We had a lovely decommissioning service for the Beloved Community Commission in which all who had worked so hard were shown appreciation. They were given special wall hangings that we had an artist design, as well as the blessings of the bishop. It was moving to be closing out this part of our work knowing it would be enveloped in a larger work that was going to impact the wider church. So many times, when we close down things in the faith community, it is because they have outlived their viability, and they are basically buried. In this case, we were having what seemed akin to a funeral, but it was a resurrection at the same time, as the work would live on in the new center. The commission had done wonderful work, and some of us were going on to this new and larger work. It was a moment to be reflected upon in more than a casual manner.

One day, early on, when I was sitting in my office thinking about all the work I had taken on by becoming the executive director of the Center for Racial Healing, I realized I was failing retirement quite well. I was taking on more work than I had done my last years as a professor. It was clear that I was not going to be a craftswoman, herbalist, folk medicine practitioner, or anything other than a very busy person trying to give life to the vision I had called the Center for Racial Healing.

The other side of the coin for me was that we had opened this lovely place and made grand statements about who we were and what we would do, and after the fanfare of opening and the declarations of intent that were made, everyone left but me. I did not have any staff for the first couple of months. I came to that big empty space each day for those lonely months, truly wondering what I had gotten myself into. Of course, we had our ongoing workshops on dismantling racism that I was helping to lead. We also had a few online book studies. However, beyond that, we were not close to being a center. We had much developmental work to do to create a full-fledged center with a slate of programs and other activities. Our work was a tall hill to climb.

But it did not take long. I had the great opportunity to hire a young seminary student to work as an intern. We set ourselves to the task of developing our first year of programs. My intern eventually became a part-time campus missioner while continuing to work part-time for the center. By the beginning of the next school year, I had an administrative person and the intern, which was great. Then by our third year we had a program manager, and that brought staff up to two full-time people and a contractor. We kept adding interns and others to help us get the work done.

The Center for Racial Healing has opened doors for me to do the work I have dedicated my life to doing for the past fifty years and will continue to do until I am not able any longer. I am so proud of what we have done throughout the wider Episcopal Church across the United States and beyond. We have worked with other faith communities as well, and our programs have been engaged by people in Europe, Canada, West Africa, Australia, Honduras, and the Dominican Republic.

Along with this, we hosted an international women's empowerment conference, which brought together women from fifteen countries in Latin America. This conference was the second one we did, and it was designed to be a part of a larger project to help those in attendance find more sustainable ways to live. The conference grew out of my desire to keep my promise to my sisters in Latin America that our center would not forget them and that we would work to include them in as many ways as possible.

Even when I was a child frightened of storms and speeding cars, I had to have known there was more for me than fear. I have always been staring at the horizon, wondering what is beyond the things I can see. Sometimes, as a young girl, when I sat out back watching the sun rise, I felt a sense of call. My family saw it too. Since they were not trying to be too analytical about it, some of them simply said I had "wheels in my head" because I was ready to go anywhere, anytime I had a chance. But when I retired, I thought that most frontiers had been scanned and visited. It was shortsighted of me to think that all my heavenly directors were finished with the work they had in mind for me.

I encountered ageism again when I turned seventy-five. Some folks began mumbling about when I was going to retire from running the center. Well, it was important to put an end to that conversation, which I did in no uncertain terms. I promised to lead the center for five years, which I am doing as I write this book. I will be vacating the executive director position by the time this book is published in 2024. I have many more frontiers to visit. I have found that out over the past five years.

As executive director, I have worked harder than I ever worked before because there is such a varied array of tasks to manage. Over these past years, I have raised over two million dollars, which has sustained the center quite well in these formative years, though more money will need to be raised as the center continues to live into its full potential. These years have been challenging but also enlivening. I have learned many new ways to see and to do things. My prophetic voice is stronger than ever. I am clearer about my reason for being in the world, and I have more courage to speak out of that space than ever before. It has been affirming to realize that I am beloved by the Creator and trusted to be the steward of many gifts and treasures that are to be shared as widely as possible.

That little girl from Arkansas who didn't know if she had a place in this world discovered her voice. When I wrote my first book, it was titled *I Want Somebody to Know My Name*. My goodness, I couldn't have been clearer about wanting to find my voice. I remember my first therapist telling me after he read my book that it was clear I wanted to be loved. I was taken aback by his comment since that is actually the only thing he had to say about my book, and I was looking for a compliment, I think. I have had a lot of years since 1978 to think about what he said. He was right. I was always searching for love. I didn't know it in the beginning. But it is clear to me now. I am so thankful I got the message that the search would be better and bring more satisfaction to my life if I tried to be a loving person as I searched.

So much of my navigation of these frontiers simply seemed like an effort to survive under circumstances that were often desperate. As the mother in Langston Hughes's poem "Mother to Son" declares, "Life for me ain't been no crystal stair." I was the daughter of a sharecropper, and I worked in the fields. I grew up under racial terror and segregation. I faced rheumatoid arthritis and raised two brilliant Black boys on my own. I made my way in academia despite the negative energies directed at me and innumerable early educational deficits. And now I am traversing this new frontier that has brought the chance to lead the Episcopal Church and any others who are interested in the work of racial healing. This is a different staircase from any I have known. I am not sure whether it is crystal or not, but it is different.

This frontier has made me both teacher and student. I have been heartened by the power of my voice and the manner in which it has been received as I have tried to help create a livable and sustainable world for everyone on the planet. This livable and sustainable world must necessarily be free of racism as well as classism, sexism, homophobia, and other oppressive structures. When we have created such a world, then we will have the Beloved Community. Everyone talks so much about this Beloved Community, but they seem confused about the path that can lead to its birth. To me, there is a clear path forward; it is only a question of whether we want to walk it.

I have also been disheartened many times. I was very disheartened when I went to the 2018 General Convention of the Episcopal Church and learned of the competition and outright jealousy expressed by some of the folks there who had been engaged in work around race for decades and somehow saw the Center for Racial Healing as a threat. What an unfortunate idea to hold in a world where there is enough racism to last for many millennia, and which could use all the energy that all of us who are trying to do this work could find and much more. There was not going to be a shortage of work. But the human propensity to focus on scarcity was quite alive and well for these individuals. People passionately objected to our

changing the language from "antiracism" to "racial healing."
The naysayers tried to discourage participation in the dining
room luncheon our center was hosting at the convention,
which, despite their efforts, was a very successful event.

This was all very instructive to me. There are so many
people who should be worrying about racism and inequal-
ity but instead are worrying about scarcity, competition, or
just what others are doing. They feel threatened instead of
seeking to give love, find love, and bring as much healing
as possible to whatever space they have a chance to occupy.
I made a clear decision to be inclusive, to invite everyone
to the table. We had invited the whole Episcopal Church to
send representatives to a series of gatherings to explore how
a center such as the one we were charged with establishing
could be helpful to them when we first opened, and many
dioceses did send folks. Many did not. Most of the people
who were worried about our existence chose not to accept
our invitation. But I kept employing the remedy I knew how
to access. I worked to keep an open heart and kept reaching out to folks until it became obvious that their position
against us was more important than the work and they had
no intention of changing their minds or their behavior. I left
them alone and kept working.

I understand how it feels to be left out. As a Black woman,
I have been left out and made invisible. I have been seen as
someone to be frightened of and someone to keep at a safe
distance. I have been passed over for things I thought I deserved and have been subjected to the daily microaggres-
sion that simply comes with living in the United States in
a Black body. So I understand how some of those folks felt.
They wanted a center, and we were the ones with it. But this
work is larger than all of us, and it deserves to have us put
our fragility away so that we can engage the many challenges
that stand between us. The only option is to keep an open

heart and to stand firmly in living as much of the best truth and best parts of our vision that we can.

I am certainly not always able to be magnanimous, and it is especially difficult when I am doing new things that are challenging my courage quotient. I had to work on not spending too much energy on the negative things being said about us. It is good to be seventy-five years old and have a good track record to stand on. No criticism matters these days unless someone is genuinely trying to help us improve the excellent work we are already doing. It will be a great honor for me to leave this work knowing that we have the solid foundation of a six-year history and a grand reputation to continue to build on, and affirmation from hundreds of people across the globe about the positive impact of our work.

We have a vision at the Absalom Jones Episcopal Center for Racial Healing about being a brave space where we tell the best truth we can discern. We also don't try to make the truth anything more than it is. This truth-telling spirit helps us do our work better, and it brings more possibilities for authentic relationships to develop between those who come through our doors. So many people have spoken to us about creating a "safe space" for racial healing work to occur. But often, we have to be willing to step into dangerous territory. We have to take risks. This frontier has demanded bravery from me, and I have passed on that understanding as much as possible in regard to all the programs, conversations, podcasts, and blog posts we have produced. We want to highlight bravery in this culture of fear. We need to move away from behavior that is based on avoiding whatever is fueling our deepest fear. Instead, we need to act out of courage and conviction to make the world more livable, and we designate the space that we have created as " brave space" where this work can occur.

10

Silence, Journals, and Dreams

SOME READERS MIGHT WONDER HOW I have been able to sustain myself on my journey from fear to empowerment. Others might wonder what daily practices have allowed me to do the prolonged, difficult work of racial healing. Still others might wonder how, in a life full of twists and turns, a person might learn to discern the most meaningful and life-giving path. People living with pain, like my own rheumatoid arthritis, might want to know how they can find joy in desperate circumstances. Throughout my life, I have traveled through different spaces and come to understand their energies—both those that are in the open and those that are more hidden. Here I will share some of the helpers I've encountered along the path. Today, our world is noisier than ever. There are so many voices that it's difficult to discern which ones are speaking the truth. Throughout my adulthood, silence—which initially was my defense against what I could not understand—has become an important discipline and help. So has journaling, which, like silence, opens up the space that allows inner wisdom to thrive. Finally, the work of Carl Jung has deeply impacted my personal and professional lives. Connecting with his work has helped me access the deeper meanings and messages of my dreams. In doing so, I have found yet another path from fear into freedom.

It has been asked, "Is there enough silence in the world that the voice of God can be heard?" This is a very good question for the world at large, but it resonates amazingly well with me as I attend to the noise in my own head and heart. In an effort to quiet personal noise, I have practiced the discipline of silence for many years. I have spent fifteen years living without television in order to help create more silence in my external world. Before, there were times when I allowed the television to provide an escape for me. It became clear that the best remedy for me was simply to live without it.

Silence has been attractive to me for much of my life, but finding a way to make it a routine practice has taken much effort and intentionality. In 2009, I spent the entire year taking one day a week to go to my church and spend the day in silence. I began this exercise after I vacated the house I had owned in Macon and lived in for twenty-five years and moved into an apartment that was half the size but that was right next door to my church, St. Francis Episcopal Church. I had begun to feel the energy of Atlanta drawing me. I was on a mission to discover what was next, and I had to find a way to hear what my heart really desired and not allow myself to choose something only because it was time for a change. I had been a participant, leader, designer, and sponsor of silent days and retreats. But the space I was entering at this time seemed particularly daunting.

It quickly became clear that it did not matter how much I had read about, participated in, or organized silent days. Of course, my past practice helped me to imagine the path in the first place, but new layers of discipline and determination were required. This discipline and determination would be given by grace, as is the case with all things spiritual.

As part of my move from a three-thousand-square-foot house with an attic and garage to an eleven-hundred-square-foot apartment, I relieved myself of half of my possessions. Then I embarked on going to St. Francis's each Tuesday morning at nine and staying in the church in silence until five. My rector teased me about becoming an anchoress like Julian of Norwich. The anchoress is enclosed in a cell, which cannot be voluntarily vacated. Her intention is to live a life of prayer and contemplation. Though I began reading Julian of Norwich with a fellow parishioner, I had no intention of becoming enclosed in a cell. It was not a simple matter to walk on the path of silence I had laid out for myself, but it was clearly the correct path for me at the time.

The freedom that came from downsizing was a tremendous gift. I remember that even though my house had a new roof, there had been a small leak in the den, probably caused by the wind blowing off shingles. I had become so upset about that because the roof was fairly new. Since I was moving, I let it go. After I got settled into my apartment, I woke up to a massive rainstorm one night; I felt great when I realized I didn't have to concern myself about the rain because I no longer had to worry about maintenance. The relief almost took my breath away. I had not realized how large the burden of the house had been for me until I let it go.

This new period of downsizing and engaging silence in such an extended manner was lonely. I did not spend a lot of time talking to others during this time. I found it easier to choose solitude. During this time, I had many cat visitors. There was a serious problem with uncared-for cats in the apartment complex, and my patio became a rest stop for many of them. I took many of them to the no-kill shelter in Atlanta. I also found other long-term homes for many of them. It became another joke among my friends that the word was out in the cat universe about my house being the place to go for refuge. The irony is that I did not really like cats and had thought myself too allergic to their hair to have them around. But somehow there was a major shift for me around all this. I read Julian of Norwich and thought about her living as an anchoress with her cat. And then I was provided an opportunity to choose a little homeless kitten. I did it without much thought. I called her Little Julian, and she has been my companion for the past twelve years. One of the most important things I learned during this time is the importance of being kind to yourself while practicing a discipline. I learned it was important to allow a day that is committed to being silent to unfold instead of trying to map it out. I took naps, I walked the labyrinth, I sat in our lovely sanctuary, I walked a bit on the grounds, and I rocked in our wonderful rocking chairs.

I began to look forward to being away from the computer, the phone, and my many conversations and commitments on these days. It became easy to hold people in my heart because I had space to allow them to be present to me. I'm glad that gift has stayed with me. Even though I am not currently having whole days of silence, I am able to hold people in my heart and walk with them regardless of how many demands are being placed upon me in other arenas. I do this by paying attention to how my attention gets turned toward a person I need to pray for or message. I have learned not to ignore those internal promptings and thoughts that come because they are meant to be acknowledged.

As I moved through the year of silence keeping, it became clear to me that it was time to move from Macon, which I noted earlier. Silence helps to open up space for me to hear what cannot be heard when I am not practicing silence as a discipline. It is important to note that often those who don't walk close enough to us on our paths to see our evolutionary patterns might see our actions as abrupt and perhaps impulsive at times. However, closer examination might reveal that these patterns may be resulting from deep and long-term self-interrogation and much effort to discern what is next. Some of my friends were mystified about my move from Macon to Atlanta after I had lived in Macon for over forty years. Some of them predicted that I would become depressed and might discover that I had made a huge mistake. Actually, I was never depressed about moving to Atlanta. It was not a mistake, and I have not spent even one-half of a millisecond regretting it. It was one of the best things I have ever done for myself. I continue to wake each day with the utmost gratitude for the grace that gave me the courage to take this step.

Along with the discipline of silence, I have engaged in serious journal keeping. I have kept a journal for the past fifty years. I enjoy beautiful bound books of empty pages more than anything else I can name. I have journals of all shapes and sizes. I have bought many of them myself, but my family and friends enjoy giving them to me because they know how much I enjoy them. The most amazing ones have come from my sons. They are so good about knowing how to choose the best gifts for me, and when it comes to journals, they seem to have an extra-special sense for what I love.

I have kept gratitude journals along the way in order to remind myself not to take for granted the many small daily blessings I receive, such as an unexpected phone call that inspires, or even just fresh, clean water to drink or good air to breathe. Then there are my numerous dream journals. Along with these are the journals that simply hold my daily reflections on life as I have tried to make sense of so many things and live faithfully in the midst of challenges. I have written about arthritis and my long and vigilant effort to keep myself mobile. I've written about all the challenges I've had to face with my experience of pain and disability. The list is endless, and I have boxes of journals to bear witness to my discipline of recording my thoughts in writing over the past decades. The process of journaling has saved me a lot of pain because in a journal, I can say whatever I wish without backlash. I work through issues that do not need to engage others and often find my way to clarity regarding things that are so murky. I can dialogue with myself about things I don't wish to discuss with other people. This avoids unnecessary drama in life, because the conversation stays on the page.

My journals are also containers for the dreams and hopes that need to be held in my heart and savored. Joys, triumphs, and many other threads that need to be followed or acknowledged find their way into the conversation I am having with myself in the pages of my journal. My journals are my closest companions, and quite honestly, I am not very anxious to part with them yet. I read many of the earlier ones as I prepared to write this book, and I was taken by surprise at the energy emanating from them.

My journals are waiting for me to find them a home, and that is among the next major projects I have to turn my intention toward. My sons have been clear about their desire for me to be the one to find a home for my journals for when I have moved on to the next iteration of life. They do not wish to have the responsibility of them. It is not easy to make a decision about what to do with belongings that are so intrinsically connected to someone. Thus I want to act kindly toward my sons by not leaving my journals for them to have to manage when it is time for me to go to the next life. I have been invited to place them in a few archives, and I will make a decision about that sooner rather than later.

The journal is such a container of life and a record of all the pieces of love we carry. These pieces, like the scraps that made up my mother's quilts, seem useless until their meanings are revealed. Once they are sewn together, they become a beautiful whole. On the pages of a journal, it is possible to see how these scraps of love interact with one another. Once I see the pattern, it is difficult to imagine them being anyplace except here, on these pages. Years ago, I was not as aware of how precious my journals were to me. When I traveled, I would pack my journal as I did any other books. On one trip, the airport misplaced my luggage for a day or so. My journal was in my luggage. It felt to me as if I had left one of my children someplace. I woke up in the night feeling as if I had lost something or someone who was very special to me, and I found myself in tears. It was then that I realized how much I was connected to that record of my life. I was so relieved when the airline's representative called to tell me my luggage was located and was being sent to my home. I have never put my journal in my checked luggage since that day. Now, my journal travels in my handbag, or it stays at home.

Sometimes my journals focus on the content of my dreams. When I encountered Carl Jung's work, I found that it gave me language for some of the experiences I had previously not had language to express. It helped me to make sense of the unnamed fears I had been navigating for a long time. Jung helped me to see the fallacy in trying to be a loving, kind, productive person in the world without understanding what the foundation of my life was built on. He helped me to begin to ask much better questions of myself, my history, my faith, and all the narratives I had used to help me. From Jung, I learned that I wanted to mine the richness of my own soul. I also learned to use his lens, which engages the conscious and the unconscious, for understanding my experience.

I learned how to pay attention to my dreams as an adult, using better tools to make sense of them than I had as a child. As a child, I shared my dreams most mornings and got very literal interpretations of them from my parents. Those parental explanations sufficed for that time and at least helped me to be very open to using dreams as a resource.

During all my college years, I had numerous dreams that involved being chased, hounded, and hunted by dark forces that meant to do harm to me. I knew they were going to harm me, and I was always working to escape from buildings and hiding in dark places. Even when I found hiding places, it was difficult to find openings when I tried to leave them. I was not keeping a dream journal at this time. I wish I had been. But even though those dreams happened more than fifty years ago, I can still remember some of them. I don't remember them in detail, but I recall the feeling and tone, as well as the overall impression of trying desperately to save myself. Those dreams were trying, without much success, to get me to seek a healing path that I didn't know how to find. When I was a student at Compton College, I tried to get counseling, but by the time I was removed from the wait list, it was too late for me to access the counseling. Then when I transferred to Pepperdine, I dove into my work, religion, and trying to save the world. I pretty much forgot about trying to save myself. I didn't realize what a grave mistake that was, but I was a young woman on a vigilant search for meaning in general and my meaning in particular. I was also scared about not making it in the world. This made me work even harder to make sure that I did indeed make it.

When I moved to Georgia and began working at Mercer, I discovered Jung and decided to find a good therapist to help me work with these dreams of distress. Now that I was a working professional, though I was still searching for a deeper and better understanding of myself, I was able to be more fully committed to my inner work because I had been seeking the light since I was a little kid getting up before daybreak to watch the sun rise.

My interest in Jung came from a longing to connect with my dreams. I had read many writers who kept referencing Jung, and I knew I needed to read him for myself. It was recommended that I begin by reading his autobiography, *Memories, Dreams, Reflections*. I took the advice and bought the book. It was not an easy read because Jung assumes the reader has a background that would make it possible to clearly understand the wide range of material and thoughts he was presenting, which were so matter-of-fact to him because of his long-term research and work. It took me a good while to work through the book, and I had to look into other sources at times to understand him better. But I did that with great care because I really wanted to understand.

After I had been reading the book for a few days, I started to feel that I was in a conversation with others about it, though I was not. There were times when I could almost hear someone speaking to me. It was a bit akin to dreaming, and I could almost hear the conversation but not quite. That feeling got stronger the deeper I got into the book. The sense of being in a conversation continued, and I began to sense that I was being accompanied by someone. It was not frightening to me, but it was a bit disconcerting. I would be standing in a store, and it would seem that someone was there, but I didn't see anyone. I paid attention and kept doing all that I had to do. I continued to be very busy teaching at a women's prison in a program that Mercer had initiated, and I was working full-time as assistant dean of women, engaging with students around programming, counseling, and whatever else they needed me to do. I didn't have a lot of time to read, but I read in the evening as much as I could. I carried the book with me everywhere I went, and if I had a few free minutes, I would read it. It was clear that it was important to get this book read.

I was getting close to finishing the book. It was my night to travel the thirty miles from Macon to Milledgeville to teach at the women's prison. But when I got there, the evening head count had not come out correctly. This was a part of the ritual of prison life. Two times a day there was a count to make sure everyone was accounted for. If it didn't come out right, everyone had to stay where they were until the count was corrected. On this particular night, they seemed to have more trouble than usual because it took a long time for them to finish. That was a part of the frustration of teaching there, because if it took thirty, forty-five, or sixty minutes, we lost that class time. It wasn't easy to make up the time because classes met once a week. But I had my Jung companion, which is how I regarded the book by this point. I sat and read for the entire time. I finished just before they got the count corrected, in the dingy, poorly lit library at the women's prison. Just as I read the last lines and closed the book, I felt what seemed like someone walking past me. Though I didn't see anyone, I had a clear sense of someone leaving the room. I had never felt that type of presence before and I have never felt it again, even though I've read many books that have affected me profoundly. Neither have I had the experience of feeling as if I were in a series of conversations that were not conscious enough for me to really hear what was being said but that were more than background noise. It was an amazing and unusual experience.

I knew not to pretend that it didn't happen. For me, understanding Jung was not about just adding one more thinker to my intellectual arsenal. This particular body of knowledge had something to do with my way of being in the world and the work that I would do for the remainder of my life. I didn't know that at the time, but it became clearer as I continued in my studies. I flirted with the idea of going to Zurich to study Jung's approach. After realizing that was not the best idea for me, I considered going to one of the C. G. Jung Institutes in the US to become an analyst, but that was not it either. Like so many other things that I have engaged, I would become an itinerant Jungian.

Some of my white male colleagues at Mercer, who were particularly paternalistic and sure they knew what I should be doing as a young African American, mused about what made me pursue Jung. They voiced how difficult it was for them to understand why I wasn't studying some great Black scholar instead. I was rather angry when I heard about this, but it was not worth the investment of too much energy. They were not clear about what their own work was; had they been, they would not have had time to muse about my life. After all, it was my brain to use as I chose. Those white men who felt that they had the authority and the right to concern themselves with my life and work had no earthly idea about the inner journey I was embarking upon and how far away from the truth about me they were. They had decided what my place should be. Since I defied their paternalism by deciding I was going be a scholar, then they thought they knew exactly what kind of scholar I should be. It was this type of thinking that had hounded Black folks for decades. It was the reason preaching and teaching were seen as the only vocations for Black folks, along with being morticians. I would prove them wrong by getting my PhD and thinking whatever I wanted to think and pursuing any intellectual thread I desired.

My limited knowledge of Jung was helpful as I began therapy, which went quite well. After seeing a therapist for quite some time, I noticed that I had the frightening chase dreams less frequently. During this time, I had a dream in which I was wounded and left on the side of the road. In the dream, I did not know how I was going to get any assistance, and I was very afraid and felt very much in danger. I was in front of a Mercer University building that had a very busy street running in front of it. As I lay there, a dark army green jeep came up to me with a big red cross on it, indicating that it was carrying a medic. Two people got out, picked me up, and took me with them. I woke up from that dream and never had one of those frightful dreams again, although I had been experiencing them for years. Since I had this dream in 1978, I have not had a dream where I was chased or frightened. In fact, I have had no dreams with frightening tones. It seems clear to me now that the cycle of chase dreams was to help me move forward into dream work and therapy.

Dreams can be such a profound source of healing. I didn't really need to talk about this dream. I had a sense in my entire body and soul that it was about a major turning point for me. I was correct. I had learned how to keep a dream journal by this time, so I wrote this dream down with the intention to work on it with my therapist, but it needed little work because it spoke to me so deeply. Even though it was decades ago, it is almost as vivid in my mind when I think or talk about it now as it was when it happened. There are often dreams like this, which have a specific message that needs no analysis or very little because the message is so clear.

There is one other dream you must hear about because it has informed the courage I've found for living in this world of uncertainty. The following dream came during another time of impending transition, toward the end of 1998, when I was so weary and so thirsty for change and a respite from the daily grind of my life. It remains quite vivid in my memory. In the dream, I was in my bedroom, which was covered by monarch butterflies. There were butterflies on the ceiling, on the walls, on my bed, on the floor—not one inch was uncovered. At first, my dream self was frightened about them, but the fear quickly dissipated and I became curious about them. Finally, I was comforted by their presence. I realized in the dream that I was being sent a very powerful and empowering message. I awoke from the dream feeling as if I needed to get ready for major change. A few weeks later, I received a call from the president of Mercer inquiring about whether or not I would have any interest in becoming a loaned executive to the mayor of Macon, which began the work described earlier and led to my work at Wesleyan and into my current work, so it is relatively easy to see the powerful messaging in that dream of butterflies, with their symbolism of transformation and change. I had been so ready for a change but was not sure how to orchestrate it, given my current circumstances. I was delighted.

The gift of my new position with the mayor was both a source of great gratitude to me and very humbling. I was not used to anything being easy. When things seemed too easy, I was suspicious about how long they would last and worried that they may not last at all. The dreams and experiences I've described in this chapter are actually quite consistent with my understanding of the world as being grounded in both the physical and the spiritual. There is a legitimate reason to expect assistance to come from many sources as I walk this path from birth to death. Thus it should not surprise me when that energy presents itself. But, since it is mystery, perhaps what I am really experiencing is wonder more than surprise.

In addition to silence, dream interpretation, and journaling, my creative expression is an integral part of how I maintain my sanity. You know that I have enjoyed making greeting cards. Now that I am no longer thinking I will become a craftswoman, I make my cards for friends and family. I enjoy using handmade paper and all types of materials, such as buttons, dried flowers, stickers, paints, and wax, to create these little pieces of art. In the past few months, I have been working with tea- and coffee-stained paper, which looks as if it is aged, as well as painting mandalas as another way to symbolize wholeness and healing. I can spend a day making one card at a time. I enjoy the way I am able to focus on a project and stay with it until it is finished, regardless of how long it takes. This is another gift that has been supported by the disciplines of silence and journaling.

On another note, I want to share how much I enjoy ironing, which I have only very recently recognized as a contemplative practice for me. When I was the primary ironer in our house as a youngster, I liked doing it, and it took me all day to iron all the clothes for everyone. But it was more a chore that had to be done, and I was the one to do it. I liked that at the end of the day, I could see what I had accomplished, but I did not think much about it beyond that. Now, I realize that sitting and ironing allows me the freedom to be in many places without moving from my chair. I can pray for people and reflect on many things that I might not otherwise manage to think about it. Ironing is slow. It doesn't require much attention, but it does require a bit. It occupies a portion of my mind, but there is a lot of space for thinking and sorting. Ironing and quilting are related for me in this regard.

As I think about the quilting bees that my women elders engaged in when they were younger and I was a child, they were certainly support groups for those who came to participate. The women had to pay some attention to what they were doing, but there was plenty of room to expand one's attention. Of course, unlike rocking chairs, which you are constantly moving in but going no place, at the end of ironing there are clothes ready to wear. At the end of a quilting project there is a new piece of art. While there does not have to be any such offering at the end of an act of contemplation, it is sometimes a neat secondary benefit to have an end product.

I have been speaking to other women of color about how they go about engaging contemplative life. All of us agree that it has been liberating for us to name things like quilting, art making, and ironing as contemplative acts. It might be tempting to dismiss some such pursuits as simple domestic tasks that have to get done. But they also have a spiritual and psychological component to them. And it is crucial to transform them into positive actions for us who had them assigned to us because we had been designated the "mules of the world" who did every task that no one else wanted to do. Raising these tasks to a higher level and seeing them in such a positive way makes it possible for them to become a generator of new and transformational energy.

My psychological and spiritual well-being are not supported by journaling and contemplation alone. I am deeply supported by a cloud of witnesses. The writer of Hebrews does an amazing job making sure we understand that we need to have a cloud of witnesses to help us make it through this land. Black women especially travel through many valleys and other challenges to our sense of self and our faith. For years I read those lovely words in Hebrews without realizing that while they were beautiful and slightly helpful, I could have more help if I had my own cloud of witnesses. I do have them now. A handful of them live on the wall in my office at the Center for Racial Healing. They are Sojourner Truth, Harriet Tubman, Mary McLeod Bethune, Ida B. Wells, Fannie Lou Hamer, and my mother.

These women watch over me each day and make it clear to me that nothing that happens to me on any given day will ever be close to the challenges they had to face for most of their lives. They could not have imagined me and the amazing life I have. They could have never envisioned my educational opportunities and the ways in which I have a chance to engage the world. For instance, my own mother graduated from college the year that I graduated from high school. She spent eighteen years working on getting a bachelor's degree. I got a BA, MSW, and PhD in twelve years. Mary McLeod Bethune and Ida B. Wells had many challenges, including the lack of available schools and the distances they had to travel to get to the schools that did exist, as they tried to get little bits of an education. Fannie Lou Hamer went to school only until the sixth grade, and Harriet Tubman and Sojourner Truth could not read or write. While working as a spy for the Union army, Harriet had to hustle for food because they would not feed her. So life for them was far less than a crystal stair; it was often a very thorny briar patch that they learned how to navigate. Their courage informs me and my journey.

My cloud of witnesses will tolerate my short fits about wrongs that are being done to oppress people today. But they help me to realize rather quickly that I have to get up, brush myself off, and get back to the task at hand. These women help keep me focused on my real work. It is one of the blessings of my day to sit in their presence. I sit with pride and thanksgiving, but I also sit with the mandate to "hold to the difficult." I do not go running off trying to escape whatever shows up on my path or trying to organize my life around what is easy. I sit with their blessings and another mandate: do not grow weary because there is much to do. It is remarkable to be in their daily presence and to know that they are a part of my cloud of witnesses. They helped me to find the God/Goddess/Creator/Spirit/Jesus/connection to ancestors that I almost missed because I was not searching in the right places. I am thankful for the guidance.

In addition to this cloud of witnesses, I enjoy frequent communion and companionship with my sisters in the Society of St. Anna the Prophet. The Society of St. Anna is made up of a vowed group of Episcopal women fifty years old and above who live independently of one another but share many aspects of their lives. My Anna sisters came into my life in 2018 when I was in deep need of a more intentional community.

I spent a fair amount of time in the early 1980s considering joining a convent because I wanted to have a more tightly knit community than I had in my parish. It finally was clear to me that I was not really ready to live in that type of environment, though my need for deeper community and structure was quite apparent. Learning about the Society of St. Anna is yet another example of the ways in which the wall that looked solid revealed its windows and doors. The Spirit knows what is needed and does the work of bringing the best remedies. I was invited to speak for the Annas about the racial healing work I was doing. When that invitation arrived, I really didn't know who they were. I came and gave my presentation and was so amazed at the sense of appreciation they showed for me and what I had to say. I felt as if I had found home. It was a Sunday afternoon, and someone invited me to join them for lunch later that week. I was happy to do that. I wanted to learn more about them.

I had missed the deadline for applying to the society. However, the more I shared—and especially when I shared about the previous consideration I had given to joining a convent—the more I caught their attention. I was invited to apply to be considered as someone who would begin the journey of discernment with them.

I was elated, and surprised that they had even found me. Though I had seen the Annas before in their vestments at some of the ordinations and other services at the Atlanta cathedral, I didn't know really know who they were. I was most humbled and encouraged. This affirmed that my heart hunger for deeper community had been answered, and in a particular manner, even though this was not the subject of any prayer I had ever uttered. When I connected with my St. Anna sisters, I recalled that Howard Thurman said in one of his interviews that the person who is praying is always answered. He didn't say that whatever you pray for you will get. In this case, I had not verbalized the prayer in my heart; I don't know what words I would have even said. The prayer merely manifested as deep hunger, and I was answered. Now I sat in the room with these women who would become extended family for me. I could not have begun to imagine this on the Sunday, six months before, when I pulled into the driveway to tell them about the racial healing work I was shepherding.

What drew me so instinctively to the St. Anna sisters? It was not better sermons, different music, more variety in the classes, greater expressions of commitments to justice, racial healing, or even seeking deeper connections to God. Those were not the missing elements. It was their ongoing engagement with one another, their creation of a space where we women can discuss, disagree—argue, if need be—challenge one another, and share our faith, fears, hopes, joys, triumphs, failures, shortcomings, brokenness, strengths, and weaknesses without having to worry about how we will be perceived the day after we have shared. The bond between us is strong enough to stand whatever truth needs to be told. I cannot say any of this about any parish I have ever had the good fortune to be in. Along with this, we are a community who practices the vows of simplicity, creativity, and balance. We are careful to live our daily lives in a manner that honors our vows.

I happen to believe that the communities we call churches are supposed to be places that are brave enough to live the love that is described in 1 Corinthians 13. I believe that we are to be able to bear all things with one another and to hold one another up. We can foster strength on the days we are weak and give hope when we are feeling less than hopeful. I believe that standing together is the only place to stand. When we allow our ego to dictate anything other than this type of care and love for one another, we are standing against all that the Creator hopes for us. Now that I have caught glimpses of this type of community with my Anna sisters, I am more convinced than ever.

11

Scraps of Love

A S I SAID EARLIER, THE BEAUTY OF QUILTING is watching how old garments can be cut into small pieces and transformed from their worn and even unlovely state into a magnificent quilt. These pieces of cloth were once in good shape, but once they become ragged, they no longer have a clear purpose in the eyes of the world. And yet, they have a larger purpose. These scraps of love, woven together, become a new invention, a quilt. We witness a similar phenomenon in the psychological and spiritual arenas of life. We can take all our narratives, encounters, triumphs, failures, hopes, and fears and allow them to be woven into a fabric that represents our journey. Each individual piece might not be beautiful or have a clear purpose. But together they become a unified whole, both useful and beautiful.

This process describes the path my life has followed. Some of my experiences have been the source of great wounding, others have been inspiring, many have taught me great lessons, and others have demonstrated how much I still have to learn. But all of them woven together have created the person I have become and will continue to become. None of them can be valued too much above another, though some of them were more pleasant than others. All of them made necessary contributions to my overall growth and development.

Now, I reflect on all these pieces of my life. I think about my earliest years, when I was that little girl running through the black walnut grove, from my house to my grandfather and aunt's house. I think about the journey I've been on from that place to who I am now—the crone, the wise elderly woman, whose voice has become respected in racial healing work across the United States and in several other countries. I cannot think of any period in my life to which I wish to return. I am delighted to be here today. I am thankful to have the opportunity to continue to enjoy the journey of discovery as I see more parts of myself and gain a deeper understanding of life. I am also grateful to have so many opportunities to bear witness to what I have already discovered.

On May 22, 2022, I sat in front of a large crowd at Washington National Cathedral. I was in that space as the preacher. I was profoundly struck by what a long journey it had been from my father's sharecropping household to that day. The journey had taken me to so many places, and it had also brought me to this stage. How was it possible that the little girl who was scared of storms would become a voice of wisdom, telling people how to face their fears and speak the truth?

I can still remember the moment I was contacted by the cathedral staff.

I was surprised to be invited to preach at the cathedral, as I would not have guessed that many folks on the cathedral staff knew much about me. I didn't really know them, and I had not had any prior interactions with them. But I was invited to preach and to engage in a conversation with *New York Times* columnist David Brooks on the Monday following my sermon. As I sat there on Sunday morning, waiting to preach, I was surprised at how calm I felt. It seemed right to be there, though it also felt almost as if someone other than the person I had lived with all my life was the one to be speaking.

As I looked out across the massive crowd, I stayed close to tears the whole time. The deep sense of amazement I had about how my journey led me to this place, and about all the people who had helped me get to this day, was simply too much to bear without tears. I thought about how my father allowed me to sit on his lap all those years ago. He could neither read nor write, and yet he supported my life of the mind and my love of words. He who did not know a word of what I was reading except what I had to say about it had given me such a gift. Out of his own desperation, he provided me with hope. He was there with me that day, and he was proud of me.

I was still in recovery from my second hip replacement surgery, which had taken place six weeks before. So it was fitting for me to talk about arthritis and getting well. I talked about Jesus healing the man at the Pool of Bethesda and the profound query that Jesus addressed to him: "Do you want to be well?" At first I wondered if I should have chosen something more academic and scholarly to preach on, but then I realized I needed to speak from the depths of my soul about something that really mattered to me. So that is what I did. The response to my sermon was amazing. It has been viewed more than twenty thousand times since that Sunday. There were so many wonderful comments made to me that Sunday and later about how inspiring it was. I'm glad I talked about my long journey with my most fierce tutor, rheumatoid arthritis.

I had to have wheelchair assistance while I was there because the cathedral is huge and I was not able to do a lot of walking. It was embarrassing to need so much assistance, but rheumatoid arthritis has taught me well. If I am going to make myself available to preach and teach in person, I will have to ask my hosts to help make the experience as good as possible by providing a few amenities that would not be necessary if I had no mobility issues. This is one of the many ways life has taught me to speak up for myself.

Those who host me have always been so hospitable, taking care of my requests. There are so many ways that public life can be seductive and lead to hubris, ego inflation without regard to who you imagine yourself to be and how much you think that you are protected from it. While I work to keep balance in all aspects of my life, it is challenging to balance everything that comes with being a sought-after speaker, writer, and thinker. My willingness to be vulnerable and confessional is the basic ingredient that helps make the racial healing work I do successful. Any conversation that is designed to challenge listeners to open themselves to transformation has to be grounded in the speaker or teacher being willing to be vulnerable. One cannot stand on a pedestal and throw wisdom down to the listeners. The voice of the wisdom sharer must be accompanied by a willingness to take off one's shoes and walk a mile in someone else's, in order to help the listeners realize that we are on this journey together and that we have to help one another.

I experienced this type of vulnerability when I was invited to Honduras to work with the clergy in that diocese for a week of workshops on racial healing and justice. There I received a powerful message about humility. At first when I received the invitation, I was hesitant to accept it because I do not speak Spanish and I knew so little about Honduran culture. It didn't take long to learn that many of their problems with racial wounding mirror ours in the US. And after much assurance from my collaborative partners there that it could work, I accepted. However, I wanted to be careful not to appear to be the expert from the United States who was coming to tell them a lot of new truth that was guaranteed to fix their lives. I wanted to be vulnerable, and since I do not speak Spanish, I had to depend on others to convey my messages. I was concerned that the audience would not see me as the vulnerable, human person I am. Well, on the day I arrived, I hurt my leg getting in a vehicle that was far too high for me to jump into. By the evening, it was worse. I could barely sit and I could not lie down, so I got very little sleep over my first two days there.

The day after I arrived, I could not walk. Two of my colleagues had to carry me in a chair because there was no wheelchair available at the time. I was so embarrassed that they had to do that. I am not exactly as light as a feather, so it was challenging for them to have to pick me up in a regular chair and carry me several feet to the car. But they made it seem as if it were the most reasonable thing in the world to do. Neither of them showed anything except great concern and care for me.

Later in the day, when I was at the meeting site, someone provided a wheelchair that had been used by his mother. This was a welcome sight for me because I did not want folks having to carry me in a regular chair. But for the first two days of the retreat, I continued to be in terrible pain. I could not walk anywhere, could not sleep at night, and simply lived through what felt like a small nightmare. On the third day, I could not take the pain any longer, so we sought medical care for me. The bishop of Honduras arranged for me to be seen at a clinic that was run by one of his former students. The young physician was wonderful. His kindness to me was striking. My only concern was that they took me in to be seen before all the local folks who were in the waiting room when I arrived. I didn't like that because I don't want to be given preferential treatment, but there was nothing I could do about it because it was not my call to make. I decided to get off my little revolutionary horse and just accept the loving care I was getting and be grateful. The miracle steroid shots and painkillers afforded me my first night's sleep since I had arrived in Honduras three days before.

Though I was still not very stable on my right side for several days after returning home, at least I was able to walk into the airplane when it was time to return to the United States. Later I realized I had been the subject of a very important lesson. My need for assistance helped to illuminate me as a wounded healer. A vulnerable person. Actually, one of the local clergypersons confessed to me that she had thought I would be an arrogant "here I am with all the answers" American. She was refreshed by the fact that I did not turn out to be that person, and I was grateful not to appear so—though I would have been glad to skip the pain I endured, which certainly helped the workshop participants to see me better. The truth is, I am not a person who feels she has all the answers. But I am American, and I understand why the folks in Honduras, given their experiences with Americans, might expect an arrogant attitude from Americans. But instead of there being a sense of division, there was a strong sense of kinship between the participants and me. That sense of kinship filled the room, and a big part of it had to do with the fact that I, as the main presenter, was in a wheelchair and in need of their assistance. The distance between us was reduced much quicker than it would have been through my verbal presentation alone. I could've communicated my vulnerability with my words, but instead, I communicated it with my body. Their connection to me was demonstrated very warmly on my last day with them when I was able to walk from the door to my seat without having to use the wheelchair. They applauded. They were glad to see me feeling better. As I write this, I can still hear their applause, and it brings me tears of gratitude.

I understood that situation better later, as I had a chance to think about it. The week I spent with the clergy in Honduras—even with the pain and mobility issues, language barrier, and all—turned out to be one of the most inspiring and successful weeks of racial healing work I have done. I became a wise sister who was sharing out of a place of understanding but who was still as wounded as they were. It was beautiful and humbling to witness the confessions, the tears, the repentance, and the dedication to engaging difference in their environment as we ended our week together. I am not sure people would have been as willing to share if I had not been in such a state of vulnerability.

I would have preferred to have none of these troubles that I have described, but it is easy to me to understand that there is a profound message about humility to be embraced. Part of my response is to make space for these experiences and lessons to become a major part of my life quilt. These lessons did not just begin. In my early career at Mercer, I was hosting the writer Alice Walker for the African American studies program. I was not used to having to host famous people, and I am an introvert. I had to drive thirty miles to Eatonton, Georgia, where her mother lived, to pick her up for the afternoon talk that she was to give. I was nervous and feeling rather intimidated about having to go by myself. Quite frankly, I had no idea what I would talk about with her for over an hour. Well, I got to her mother's house, introduced myself and all, and just before leaving, I went to the restroom. Without thinking, I had left the car key in my very shallow skirt pocket. Just as I flushed the toilet, I heard the key hit the porcelain of the toilet. I could do nothing about it except watch it swirl to its watery grave. I returned to the living room, where Ms. Walker was waiting, and in my state of horror, I told them what happened. They were very gracious, and Ms. Walker's mother loaned me her car. As Ms. Walker and I entered the car to embark on the trip to Mercer, I was mortified. I so admired Ms. Walker, and I felt I had ruined the opportunity to be perceived as anything but some kind of incompetent person. But the lost key ended up shifting the energy. I forgot about my nervousness. It turned out that Alice Walker was not feeling well, and she was very understanding of my embarrassment. As a result, we became two women who needed each other in order to complete the tasks in front of us. I brought her to campus and got her situated and had to get another set of keys from the Mercer security office and drive back to Eatonton to get the university car. It all worked out. This was another important lesson in humility for me.

I carried this lesson in humility with me to the National Cathedral. It would've been tempting to think of this moment—my preaching in front of hundreds of people, from this historic pulpit—as a scrap of cloth that was bigger and brighter than any other in my quilt sack. But it was not. Instead, it was just another plain scrap of love, stitched together with the other scraps in my quilt. In these years, as I've become more visible to the public, I have made a point to emphasize all the pieces of my quilt rather than holding up only my successes. My struggle for authenticity has to stay central. It is a huge, unfortunate trap to fall into thinking that every day has to be filled with mountaintop experiences. It's true that I had the privilege to speak at the National Cathedral, to meet Alice Walker and Howard Thurman, to speak with David Brooks about the meaning of racial healing. However, expecting a continuous string of such experiences can lead to addictions, manipulation, and an inability to be content with life as it unfolds. There are so many more days of life that are relatively uneventful than there are unusual, highly charged days. When the unusual breaks through, as it did for me in 2021 and 2022, it is lovely and deserves to be acknowledged, but it has to be kept in perspective. I have come to understand that most of life is lived in the daily round of the uneventful. I have to remember that one sermon at Washington National Cathedral, an interview on television or radio, or the publication of a book does not alter the major trajectory of my life. When it is all finished, I am left with myself—every piece of myself, even the most ragged ones.

My body seems determined to remind me of this. In December 2021, I made the decision to have the first of two hip joint replacements. I was most tired of the pain that was being caused by my hip joints having no cartilage left in them. The first surgery went amazingly well, and within a few weeks I was feeling so much better. I have had no pain in my hip joint since that surgery was done. The second surgery was to be three months later, but it had to be done four months later because I have pernicious anemia and my hemoglobin became far too low. But I worked hard to get my hemoglobin improved, and in April 2022, I had the second surgery. I am grateful for the resolution of the pain, which is completely gone from both my hip joints, but I learned that it could take up to a year or more for my recovery and acclimation to the implants to be completed. These bodily trials were occurring right as I was gaining national attention for my racial healing work. Yet again, my body was a gift, reminding me to remain humble. Yet again, the scraps of pain and struggle were stitched with scraps of joy and excitement.

In the past few years, I have received this lesson—this vision of the quilt—again and again. In March 2022, just before my second surgery, I received the biggest surprise of all. I was nominated by a friend for, and subsequently received, the Joseph R. Biden Lifetime Achievement Award for Service. I was so excited about this great honor coming to me after these fifty years of staying close to the work in the trenches without much sense that any recognition was possible and certainly not seeking it; I was just trying to make a difference in the conversation on race. I almost did not believe my friend when she called to let me know that I was actually getting the award.

The day I received the award was a wonderful day of celebration at the Center for Racial Healing. Many of my family and friends were there, providing such a good time of affirmation for me. I am thankful, inspired, and even clearer about the call to stay focused and faithful. This is a bright scrap in my quilt, and yet it is still just another part of the whole.

You will recall from my sharing my butterfly dream that I am very conversant with butterfly energy and symbolism. Butterfly energy allows me to live with much greater ease and less concern about outcomes. It requires me to trust that spiritual resources are available and that they will show up to assist me. And finally, it requires me to accept without conditions that I am totally worthy and deserving of an easier life. I do not expect every scrap in my quilt to be bright and beautiful. At the same time, I know I have already put in a lot of the energy that is required to get things done. How else would I have survived navigating all that was before me as a single mom raising African American sons? How else could I have lived as a Black woman with a vision for racial healing that kept being put farther out into the public square? How else would I have sustained myself as a person living with a chronic illness? I received a message as I was recovering from my hip surgery, grieving the loss of my original hip joints, and learning to accept the new titanium joint replacements. The message indicated that it was time to move on to butterfly energy. I no longer needed the warrior woman energy that was necessary for my survival and the survival of my sons. Things do not always have to be challenging. It is all right to have peace and, at nearly eighty, an easier journey. I can take some time to rejoice in the brightest scraps of the quilt. Now that I have arrived at this point on my journey, I can hear this message and I am affirming it.

On this quiet, lovely fall afternoon as I finish writing this account of various parts of my journey, I find that this is one of the best times of my life. I have more energy than I have ever had in my life, and I am more eager to learn new things about myself, the nature of consciousness, and being human in general. I am eager to simply engage as never before with all who enter my space and to embrace the next lessons, whatever they happen to be. This, too, is part of the butterfly energy. On this day, I feel younger than ever. I realized a few months ago that my soul is not aging. That is the reason I feel younger each day. All my life has been undergirded by one central question: How can I be a free person who lives a life of freedom and contentment? The answers to that question have come to me gradually over time. During the time I was writing editorials for the *Macon Telegraph*, the answer lay in the fact that I came to terms with the necessity of telling the truth in my writing. At the time, I was dealing with bullies who sent nasty emails and made visits to the publisher trying to get me fired from writing. They spewed violence and vile thoughts in response to my columns. Yes, it was frightening, as I was not used to such vitriol being directed toward me. But I wanted to make sure the bullies did not have the last word. I would not allow them the power of controlling my behavior. Thus, in order to be free, I had to continue to write. I think that sometimes what appears to be courage is simply an unwillingness to abdicate my seat on the freedom train. I am not trying to be courageous as much as I am trying to stay free.

The work I do these days at the Absalom Jones Episcopal Center for Racial Healing often leads supporters to remark about my courage. While I do have courage and I will take a stand for what I believe without much hesitation, I am always keeping a watchful eye on the need to be free. Imprisonment of the heart and mind can come to me far quicker than

I realize. It is so easy to be held hostage by feelings, thoughts, ideas, old wounds, and doubts. It is easy to become the little girl frightened of storms, the little girl confused by the enormity of racism. This is the opposite of butterfly energy.

The deep inner work continues. It started with me as a little girl who got up in the mornings to see the sun rise and hear the birds wake up, and it will continue until I move on to the next part of the journey now and into eternity. This intention to do inner work as well as my daily practices—silence, journaling, and dream work—move me forward in my pursuit of being free. Perhaps having troubling external circumstances and shortages helped me more than I realize. It was clear early on that there were not going to be others who were trying to make my life what I wanted it to be. Toni Morrison talks about us Black women not having ladyhood, whiteness, or maleness to fall back on when things don't go as we might wish. Black women have known for a very long time that we have to take care of ourselves and that we cannot count on the external world to do that for us. When we have thought otherwise, it has only led to much unnecessary pain, suffering, and waste of energy that could have been spent in far better ways. From the time I was little, I knew that no other forces were working to make me, a Black girl, free. Only I could make myself free, and I could do it only on my own terms. This, too, is how my quilt is stitched together. The patches of suffering I have experienced as a Black woman are integrated with the patches that symbolize the freedom I've claimed for myself.

Part of that freedom comes from the evolving ways that I think of God. My early sharecropping farm life in Arkansas led me to be afraid, and God was tangled up in that fear. My deeper liberation means I have allowed God/Creator energy to be liberated as well. After all, what kind of Creator would hate their own creations and not wish to help them live the best life possible? So I have my earlier understanding of a God who is at best ambivalent toward me. Of course, there is much to be said for living by faith. I have a deep commitment to that way of seeing reality. But it is so wonderful to know that the Creator is not some kind of fragile being who cannot stand my questions, confrontation, doubt, or anger. The Creator can enter any situation with me. As I have moved toward freedom, I've left behind the idea of a Creator who is more about punishment than support and care. I now can see a nurturing and caretaking Creator who knows who I am and who is interested in my well-being and the well-being of every other creature on the planet. I am so glad to have arrived at this understanding in time to have it support the remainder of my life. And my exploration of faith has expanded into many different traditions. I am energized by the desire to learn about the ways in which my African ancestors navigated the spiritual world. I am also interested in the ways Celtic cultures and the Indigenous peoples of North America have engaged the Spirit. There is a lot to learn about the ways in which spirituality and relationship to the Spirit have been engaged by many who are a part of my legacy.

Today, my quilt is made up of both joy and pain. I recognize that this is not the end of my journey. As time goes on, new scraps of both joy and pain will be added. It is easy to be afraid of pain. Living a life of courage is not necessarily about not being afraid. Instead, it is about being committed, being faithful, and refusing to relent when things are hard. I do feel that I am on more solid ground because of solidarity with myself. I also have this solidarity with others who themselves are internally grounded. Together, we live lives of disruption because the life well lived will necessarily be disrupted. The status quo is never the final word.

I experience great pain when I am living in spaces of indecision or lack of clarity. This is sometimes called being in liminal space. This space is most prevalent during times of great transition, when you are vacating one space and headed to another. In this period, you might be sure where you are but not clear about where you are headed. Most people who are engaging their inner community will readily identify with how this feels. Though it appears that there is a bit of a void and that you are almost in a free fall, it is more than likely not that way at all. It is more likely that the space of uncertainty is in fact a place itself. You are moving from a place of clarity into a new space. When this new space is manifested, it can feel disruptive. You might even feel as if there is no place to stand. I have lived in this space so much. It feels like being on the margins instead of being in any place, and it can be frightening. It is the space that makes staying faithful and focused complicated. Of course, you might experience a strong desire to find a place that feels more stable, more secure. This place can lead you to engage in addictive behavior as you seek a remedy for the sense of being disrupted. These remedies can include food, shopping, busyness, alcohol, drugs. I learned to accept that I simply had to stand in this place of disruption, even though it felt like a death. Standing in this place is akin to dying because old ways of viewing the world and yourself have to be interrogated and often abandoned. It is tempting to look for those easy remedies. But if that temptation can be resisted long enough to move to a new place, there is great joy, hope, and rebirth.

As I move along into the next iteration of my racial healing work, I don't know where it will lead me. But I trust that it will take me to the places that are best suited for me, given what I've experienced on the journey so far. I am curious about how this butterfly energy, so newly revealed to me, will impact my racial healing work.

Today, there are no more rags in my quilting sack representing desperation. The truth is, desperation was a major piece of my quilt for many years. I watched my father live with desperation for most of his life as a sharecropper who dreamed of overcoming hardship but never had the opportunity to do so. Instead, he burned down our house—the white man's white house—looking for relief. In the end, for my father, the only relief from desperation came through death.

I have faced desperation in my own life too. But such pieces no longer dominate my quilt. I am so thankful for this fact and the realization of it. Unlike my father, I have found release from the situations that cause a sense of desperation, without having to die to get away from them. Those prayers have been answered. I am struck by the ways in which change can be so subtle that it is almost elusive. I sometimes have to sit with myself for many hours to see it. But when I do see it, there is no going back. A few recent encounters that would have caused me great angst in times past have come and gone. While I acknowledged them, they did not disrupt me. I was not even aware that the process of change was happening. This is another reason that journaling is crucial for me. It is a good place to record these subtle changes.

I want to find better paths to healing, especially in terms of race. We as human beings have found so many ways to denigrate and marginalize one another. The work that I have had a chance to do has been phenomenal, yet I am quite clear about how much there is left to do and how challenging it will be to get it done. As I think of the future of this work, I know that neither I nor anyone else who cares can afford to rest until there is a place for every human on the earth to be treated as a beloved child of the Creator. While it will not happen during my lifetime, it is a good dream to hold. I understand that the survival of the planet is connected to our doing the work of racial healing. We cannot continue to sustain this brokenness. This brokenness is against the Creator's intention for us.

An important part of my own work is sharing my own example and leading in humility. I can hold up my quilt for others to see. It might be easy for people to see my public persona, the visibility of my work. But every time I am on that public platform, I want people to see my whole quilt, my full humanity. At the end of every class, workshop, lecture, interview, book signing, award ceremony, or whatever event I appear at, I am the person I was before that event. And I have to be able to be at peace with myself when there is no one left in the room but me. I am totally clear about the importance of being able to be content. It is the only way to make sure others will find it a good experience to be with me. It is the only way people feel comfortable holding up their whole quilts too. They can point to the scraps of desperation, fear, insecurity, and jealousy as well as the scraps of joy and love. We can reflect on our common struggles and victories.

As I sat with a room filled with mostly young people on a racial healing and justice pilgrimage a few weeks ago, one of them asked me, "How do you keep doing this work without burning out?" What a good question, I thought. I went on to say that it is actually quite simple. The racial healing work and the ways that I live in the world are about finding personal liberation. Howard Thurman says that the good work we do in the world is about getting ourselves out of prison. I am working to be free, and I have learned a few things along the way. In the process of sharing those things, I work hard, and a lot of good gets done. It is not about doing a job; it is about forging a life. It is about trying to be a free person. Ultimately, it is this freedom that has stitched together every scrap of my quilt. It connects the black walnut grove to the halls of academia. It connects sharecropping to policy-making. It connects the Blackness and power of West Africa to the segregated communities of the American South. It connects the fears of the past with the butterfly energy of the future. I can see the freedom stitches running throughout my entire quilt. I thank the Creator for this journey. I thank the Creator for empowering me.